D1143313

1,001
Meditations

1,001
Meditations

MIKE GEORGE

CHRONICLE BOOKS
SAN FRANCISCO

1,001 Meditations
Mike George

First published in the United States in 2004
by Chronicle Books, LLC.

Copyright © Duncan Baird Publishers 2004
Text copyright © Duncan Baird Publishers 2004
Commissioned artwork copyright ©
Duncan Baird Publishers 2004

Conceived, created, and designed by
Duncan Baird Publishers.

Library of Congress Cataloging-in-Publication
Data available.

ISBN-13: 978-0-8118-4506-9
ISBN-10: 0-8118-4506-0

Manufactured in Thailand
Typeset in Shannon

Managing editor: Bob Saxton
Editor: Lucy Latchmore
Managing designer: Manisha Patel
Designer: Sailesh Patel
Commissioned artwork:
David Dean, Hannah Carty, and Sailesh Patel

10 9 8 7 6 5 4 3

Chronicle Books LLC
680 Second Street
San Francisco, CA 94107
www.chroniclebooks.com

CONTENTS

INTRODUCTION

In the Chinese language the word for "busy" comprises two characters – "heart" and "killer". Today, "busy" is the by-word for modern living, and it is no surprise that many thousands of hearts fail every year. Yet the true heart of each one of us lies not within the body, but within our consciousness. The spiritually minded describe it as the soul – the essence of who we are. Our spiritual well-being (our level of connection with the soul) can be measured by the quality and stability of our inner peace, and our capacity to radiate love into the world. These depend on our ability to create stillness at will. Meditation is the most effective way to promote spiritual well-being because it helps us to quieten our minds, release past hurts, be fully present, know the joy of the moment, transform the quality of our thinking and begin the healing of our hearts from inside out.

During the last twenty years I have been fortunate enough to learn and teach one of the purist forms of meditation, known as Raja Yoga meditation. Slowly but surely this practice has opened up the spiritual dimension of my life, revealing essential insights into "the self", transforming my ability to deal with the pressures of modern living, and gently healing my own heart.

Today, the word meditation has a wide variety of interpretations, ranging from thoughtful contemplation to an inner discipline of consciousness that induces profound spiritual enlightenment. In the wisdom philosophies, such as Buddhism and Taoism, meditation is viewed as a way to realize, and integrate into everyday life, certain "eternal truths" – an approach particularly valuable in the modern world, which has become fogged by illusion. Religions, such as Christianity and Judaism, include meditation alongside prayer and worship as a means to understand and personalize the spiritual truths that underpin these traditions. And most approaches to yoga employ meditation in conjunction with a variety of physical postures and breathing exercises to create a posture of consciousness that restores calm and focus. In Raja Yoga particularly, meditation involves the preparation of consciousness prior to a subtle, loving union with the source of spirit – the divine.

In creating this book I have tried to encompass a broad spectrum of possible meanings and practices of meditation, with a range of meditations, contemplative insights, nuggets of spiritual wisdom, affirmations and visualizations that I have either originated or gathered from other sources. While I personally may not fully concur with all the viewpoints

expressed in the book, I respect the original writers, whether named or anonymous. The result of this eclectic approach is not an instruction manual for meditation, but a resource of authentic and varied ways to embark upon the meditative process.

When attempting the step-by-step meditations, the secret of success is never to struggle with your thoughts and feelings. Instead, simply observe them. With observation comes a natural detachment that allows you to continue taking steps toward the heart of your self. If you are contemplating an insight or nugget of wisdom, imagine placing it in a hall of inner mirrors. This allows you to see with your inner eye the depth and breadth of that wisdom from all angles. When practising the visualizations, aim for a balance between creating the image and allowing the image to form. The key is being playful without losing the gentle concentration required to be creative.

There are a number of ways that you can use this book. One is to extract, at random, an entry per day. You can then use that entry as the focus of your morning meditation, and watch how it impacts on the rest of the day. If you have a specific need, such as a desire for more peace, you can use the index to find an entry relevant to your immediate situation. Another approach is to take one meditation per week, and practise or contemplate it daily. This deepens your experience of the meditation, triggering progressively deeper insights. Alternatively, you could pick three meditations at random, work through each one in turn, and then contemplate the interconnections between them.

Whatever approach you choose to follow, you will find that meditating regularly helps you to access and release the power of your innate peace, love and joy. This little book provides a map for this inner journey, with a thousand and one signposts pointing back to the already perfect you, and pointing forward to a more contented life lived in peace, love and celebration of the joyful spirit that you are.

If you have any questions you can contact me at mike@relax7.com.

Bon voyage, Mike George

Luck and destiny

SETTING OUT

1   **Welcoming the dawn**

In many spiritual traditions dawn – when the world is at its most peaceful – is regarded as an ideal time for meditation. Just before dawn go outside and find a place to sit and watch the sunrise. As the sun emerges above the horizon, fill your awareness with the brightening hues of the sky and rejoice in the beauty of the new day. Feel the golden rays of the sun warm your face and allow hope to fill your heart and refresh your spirit. You have started the day well.

If the weather is poor or you are unable to get a clear view of the sunrise, **visualize the dawn (2)** instead.

3   **Meeting the morning** "Each soul must meet the morning sun, the new, sweet earth, and the Great Silence alone!" OHIYESA (1858–1939)

4   **The ancient paths** "Stand at the crossroads, and look, and ask for the ancient paths, where the good way lies, and walk in it, and find rest for your souls." JEREMIAH 6:16

5   **Looking both ways** Janus, the Roman god of thresholds, provides an appropriate focus for reflection when you are embarking upon a new phase in your life. He is often depicted with two faces – one of a child looking forward into the future and one of a bearded old man looking back into the past. Visualize yourself standing in a doorway, on the threshold of your new venture. Standing beside you is Janus. Looking behind you, survey your past and ask the old face of Janus to recount the most important lessons you have gathered from your previous experiences. Then look forward and ask the young face of Janus for some positive energy for the future. Encouraged by his hopefulness, set out on your journey.

6   **Early resistance** "It is easier to resist at the beginning than at the end." LEONARDO DA VINCI (1452–1519)

7   **The forward vista** "When I look into the future, I see a vista of challenge and resolution. I venture forth with strength, hope and faith." MODERN AFFIRMATION

8   **Begin with ease** "Easy is right. Begin right and you are easy. Continue easy and you are right." CHUANG TZU (c.369–286BCE)

9   **The spirit of adventure** Approach your life as an epic adventure. Each stage of your journey presents its own particular challenges. Recognize that you have all you need within yourself to meet each challenge and embrace the lessons it brings.

10   **Starting from now** "Although no one can go back and make a brand new start, anyone can start from now and make a brand new ending." ANONYMOUS

11   **Overcoming fear** As the Russian novelist Dostoyevsky wrote, "Taking a new step, uttering a new word, is what people fear most." If you find yourself in this position, quailing on the threshold of something new, take heart, for you are not alone in your fear. Be inspired by the knowledge that others have conquered fears before you. Venture bravely into the unknown.

12   **A recipe** "Start with what you know. Mature according to nature. Let destiny do the rest." CHUANG TZU (C.369–286BCE)

13   **Life's obstacles** "For a long time it seemed to me that life was about to begin. But there was always some obstacle in the way, something to get through first, some unfinished business. Only after that would life get under way. At last it dawned on me that these obstacles *were* life." ANONYMOUS

14   **Becoming the Path** "You cannot tread the Path before you become the Path yourself." ZEN SAYING

15   **Work your loom, choose your threads** We weave our destiny on the loom of our best actions. Value this loom and keep it in good repair. Be sure that every false thread is thrown aside and not woven into the tapestry of the self.

16   **Destiny's wisdom** Once we have found the true path, destiny unfolds before us like a red carpet.

17   **Conversations with destiny** Communicating with a future self can calm the anxieties we experience in the face of the unknown. Close your eyes and imagine that standing before you is an eighty-year-old, who looks strangely like you. Encouraged by the reassuring look in their eyes, you introduce yourself. They tell you that they are the embodiment of your destiny. You converse with them, asking for advice about your life's direction. After the conversation your future self hugs you, whispering words of encouragement into your ear before slipping into the distance. Comforted by their words, you walk forward into your future with greater confidence and trust.

18   **Remember to look** "Look and you will find it – what is unsought will go undetected." SOPHOCLES (C.496–406BCE)

19   **Meditate on the waxing moon** According to Celtic tradition the waxing of the moon (when it passes from new to full) is a time of inner transformation that gives us a heightened awareness of the voice of the soul. At some point during this period, spend five minutes meditating on the moon. At the start of the meditation, imagine Olwen, the lady of the moon, assisting you in allowing your soul to speak.

20   **Life's road** "I am determined to live the full breadth of life's road as well as its length. There may be important things nestling in the hedgerows or lying neglected on the verge." MODERN AFFIRMATION

FINDING THE WAY

21 **Ask for spiritual guidance** Some people believe that we each have a number of spirit guides – angelic beings from the spiritual realm – to whom we can turn for guidance. To contact your spirit guides, address them directly, asking your question aloud, in your head, or in writing – whichever feels most natural. Remain open to the answer – it may come at any time, whether spontaneously, out of a chance conversation, or perhaps revealing itself in a book you happen to pick up.

22 **A map of life's roads** Perform this meditation to help you negotiate your way through various options. First, sketch a map of the paths available to you, and the potential paths these may lead to in the future. Illustrate each path with relevant images or symbols. Meditate on the map through half-closed eyes. Notice whether particular images draw your attention, or new images occur to you, suggesting alternative courses of action. Allow your inner sense of direction to speak to you.

   Alternatively, create a **collage of your future (23)**. Leaf through magazines, holding in mind the question "Where do I

want to go?" Cut out appealing images, stick them to some
cardboard and use the collage as a focus for meditation.

24 **Follow your star** Look for hope and guidance from your
inner star. Sit comfortably, close your eyes and bring your left
forefinger to touch the centre of your forehead, just above your
eyes. Take a few deep breaths and focus on the warmth of your
finger on your forehead. In that spot visualize a bright star
radiating energy – you may experience this as a warm, tingling
sensation. Focus on your inner star for about five minutes. Allow
it to fill you with renewed hope and purpose.

If you seek **specific guidance (25)**, ask your question silently
while focusing on your star. The answer may come immediately
in the form of words or images, or it may come later.

26 **True north** When we are finding our way, it helps to know
the nature of the experience we are seeking – our true north or
spiritual purpose. Thinking that our purpose lies in a particular
goal, such as a certain relationship or job, we may feel lost

when that option is thwarted. However, when we realize that what we are seeking is a profound experience, such as deep connection or creative fulfilment, rather than something predefined, we can seek alternative ways to live out our purpose. Meditating on the North star can help to clarify the experiences we are seeking. As you gaze at the star, ask "What fulfilment am I looking for?" and let the answers come to you.

27   **Bird migration** Each year, with the onset of Winter, flocks of birds from the Northern hemisphere fly long distances to warmer territories in the South. Birds navigate their way by following internal compasses comprising tiny grains of a mineral called magnetite, stored in their brains. During rest stops they recalibrate their inner compasses using the positions of the stars to account for the fact that magnetic north lies 1,000 miles (1,600 kilometres) from the North pole. When rest stops are too short, birds can get disorientated. In a similar way we possess a sense of inner knowing that helps us to find our way in life. But, unless we allow ourselves daily periods of time alone in which to tune into this inner knowing and recalibrate it against changing circumstances, we, like migrating birds, can lose our way.

28 **Consult the oracle** Within each of us lies an oracle to whom we can turn for guidance. Imagine entering a dimly lit room. Your oracle – a wise woman – sits at the other side of a table. You approach her and describe your dilemma. She asks you to pick three magic cards out of her fanned-out deck and lay them face-down on the table. Smiling, she begins to turn the cards over, revealing images and words that reflect on your situation. As she does so the room becomes brighter and you realize what it is that you need to do next. You thank your oracle and leave.

29 **Seeking** "Do not seek to follow in the footsteps of the ancient ones; seek what they sought." BASHO (1644–94)

30 **Commitment to the path** "I will choose my path wisely, from all the options available. I will follow my path unwaveringly." MODERN AFFIRMATION

31 **God's grace** "The wind of God's grace is incessantly blowing. Lazy sailors on the sea of life do not take advantage of it. But the active and the strong always keep the sails of their minds unfurled to catch the favourable wind and thus reach their destination very soon." MAHATMA GANDHI (1869–1948)

32 **The Spirit of the Wildwood** For Celtic shamans the image of the wildwood provides a metaphor for the world we inhabit. The shaman walks there, in his or her imagination, to acquire learning that can be applied in waking life. Imagine yourself standing in the wildwood at a place where several paths cross, uncertain which way to go. Call upon the Spirit of the Wildwood to show you your true path. Now take your first few steps along that path, first in your mind and then in reality.

33 **Signposts of the heart** "Speech and custom may be strange to me. Even the signposts of the heart are in different tongues, even in different alphabets. Yet they all point the same way: I refuse to lose myself." MODERN AFFIRMATION

34   **At a crossroads** You cannot know where you are going unless you know the path that brought you to where you are now. Imagine yourself at a crossroads. Trace in your mind's eye the path that you have taken to bring you here. Consider that path in a neutral light, neither understating nor exaggerating its hardships and wrong turnings. You cannot unwind the path of the past but you can change direction now. Choose your route and travel on in confidence.

35 **The shortest way** "Always run the shortest way, which is the way of nature." MARCUS AURELIUS (121–180)

36 **A path to be proud of** Everything we do or say has effects that ripple outward into the world – however solitary or private our actions. Try to live your life in such a way that whenever you stop and look back at the footprints you've made, you see a path that you are happy to call you own – and one that you feel others might benefit from following.

37 **Ways not taken** The way that you take is yours alone, and therefore loved. Learn to love the ways of others, so that your love for yourself does not eclipse your love for them.

38 **Reading signs** Every event that occurs, every person that appears in your life, does so for a reason. During your evening meditation replay the day like a video on the screen of your mind. Pause the video at moments that you feel are of particular importance and allow any wider significances, such as connections with other aspects of your life, to surface. Let this deeper understanding of your life inform future choices.

39 **Leave a trail** "Do not go where the path may lead, go instead where there is no path and leave a trail." RALPH WALDO EMERSON (1803–1882)

40 **A ball of light** Although we often experience intuitive wisdom, we frequently ignore its directives in order to follow reason, our own worldly impulses, or other people's ideas. Whenever you hear the quiet voice of intuition, pay attention to its advice. If rational logic conflicts with your intuition, imagine a ball of light moving from your heart and filling your mind with truth, indicating the right course of action for you.

41 **Questions of destiny** When we make a choice, is there a sense in which we are also chosen by our destiny? What is destiny, if not the choices we make? Meditate on this question, as on a Japanese koan – that is, a paradoxical question.

Unable to feel comfortable with such uncertainty, we may close our eyes to the full potential of our lives, clinging to the illusions of safety offered by habit and routine. However, to live fully we must open our eyes and accept our fears of the unknown. We must allow chance to play its part. We must take risks from time to time.

45 **Release your control** This meditation helps to ease the anxiety that can result when we are uncertain of the direction of our lives. Close your eyes and imagine rowing down a river. You try to maintain a straight course down the middle of the river, but find yourself struggling against strong cross-currents. Realizing that it is impossible to steer the boat, you allow it to drift. Amazingly, the boat does not hit either bank but is carried along by the current, leaving you free to enjoy the experience. Transfer this attitude into daily life. Try to release the need to control things in life, for some things are beyond your control. Doing so will bring you a greater sense of peace.

46 **Trusting God** "Trust God to weave your thread in the Great Web, although the pattern shows it not yet." GEORGE MACDONALD (1824–1905)

47 **Walking in the dark** "If a man wishes to be sure of the road he treads on, he must close his eyes and walk in the dark." ST JOHN OF THE CROSS (1542–91)

48   **Fortune's imagination**   Fortune is more inventive than our own imaginations. There is no point in using our rational minds to compute the infinite permutations of possibility. Let the future keep its veil and surprise us. Or else make the mind quiet and the heart content and listen for the knock of premonition.

49   **Sparks**   "Our brightest blazes of gladness are commonly kindled by unexpected sparks." SAMUEL JOHNSON (1709–1784)

50   **Questioning**   Filter your questions. There is no point in asking what is the meaning of life, only in asking how life can be lived to the fullest. The meaning of life is only known by living fully.

51   **Casting your hook**   "Chance is always powerful. Let your hook be always cast. In the pool where you least expect it, there will be a fish." OVID (43BCE–17CE)

52   **Falling plums**   "If heaven lets fall a plum, open your mouth." CHINESE PROVERB

UPS AND DOWNS

53   **A downward journey** "My journey is deep into myself, down a thousand ladders. My horizons expand with every downward step." MODERN AFFIRMATION

54   **Streams of merit** "Once I have determined to move toward enlightenment, even though at times I might become fatigued or distracted, streams of merit pour down from the heavens." SHANTIDEVA (7TH CENTURY)

55   **The inner quest** Imagine you are approaching a walled town on foot. You penetrate the outer gates and thread through a labyrinth of narrow streets. Eventually you come to a peaceful, leafy square. When life's journey seems difficult, use this visualization to give you faith that through your inner quest you will eventually find peace.

56   **Life's rodeo** "I will ride the events of my life. I have no wish to tame the laws of nature, only to show that I can stay in the saddle when my steed becomes unruly." MODERN AFFIRMATION

57   **Surf the seas of destiny** This visualization helps us to ride life's challenges with ease and grace. Imagine yourself as a surfer preparing to ride a big wave. You see the wave coming and leap onto your board in readiness, poised to catch the wave as it surges forward. As the water swells beneath you,

you respond to its momentum, aligning your board with the direction of the wave. Riding high along the breaker you feel exhilaration as the wind rushes through your hair and the cold spray douses your skin. Now visualize yourself coming safely to rest on the beach. Delight in your sense of achievement.

58   **Jason and the Golden Fleece**   Jason, one of the most famous of the Greek heroes, is renowned for his quest to capture the Golden Fleece of Colchis. During his sea voyage, Jason and his crew of fifty men encounter numerous obstacles, which they overcome through a combination of their courage and wit, and the help of mortals and gods. Face the challenges in your own life in a similar way. Surround yourself with other brave souls to travel with you on your path. Accept help offered by others and welcome gifts from the gods – that is, opportune events.

59   **Radar of the spirit**   "My intuition is the sensitive radar of the spirit. With its aid I can fly a true course through any storm."
MODERN AFFIRMATION

60 **Emotional squalls** On your journey through life there will be times when troubled feelings threaten to blow you off-course. At such times sit quietly in meditation and be aware of the storm. Watch the waves of negative thoughts and feelings as they wash over you. Accept their presence rather than trying to avoid them. By observing the turbulence, rather than identifying with it, you move into the eye of the storm – the stillness at its centre. From this vantage point, watch the storm gradually die down, replaced by the clear blue skies of a relaxed mind.

61 **Rising glory** "Our greatest glory is not in never falling but in rising every time we fall." CONFUCIUS (551–479BCE)

62 **The role of error** Error serves as both teacher and guide. From him we learn compassion for human frailty; from him we find the path that we must follow.

63 **Life-long learning** "My aim in life is to learn what I can from my experiences, to act on that learning and by my example to share what I have learned with others." MODERN AFFIRMATION

64   **Fruitful mistakes** There is an old saying that "A person who's never made a mistake has never made anything." Contemplate the fruitfulness of your past errors. What did you learn and how have these lessons shaped your life?

65   **A shared experience** Like a shoal of fish swimming as one within the ocean, humankind is bound together by a common destiny. While finding your own path in life, draw strength from the knowledge that everyone around you is also on a journey. You are never wholly alone.

66   **One step at a time** Practise this meditation whenever you feel paralyzed by fear and unable to move forward with your life. **1** Stand in the middle of a room, close your eyes and visualize the source of your fear ahead of you. **2** Bring your attention to your body. Notice how you are feeling. Breathe deeply, allowing yourself to be with your feelings without fighting them. **3** When you feel more comfortable, take a step toward the source of your fear. **4** Continue to repeat steps 2

and 3, so that by gradual acclimatization you overcome the obstacles that prevent you from moving forward.

67   **The silver lining** Hidden in the gloomiest outlook there is usually a tiny spark of hope to be found. Visualize this hope as a pinprick of light piercing the darkness. In your mind's eye move toward this light and, as you do so, watch it grow ever more powerful. Use this light to reinforce your faith that in time things will become more bearable.

68   **Divine messengers** From a spiritual perspective the difficulties we encounter serve to expand our consciousness. When problems are viewed in this light, we may feel more charitable toward those who appear to be responsible – they are simply the messengers, acting in accordance with a greater plan.

69   **Path to peace** "The well-worn path is comfortable and easy, but leads nowhere. The less-travelled path is stony and hard, but will bring me to peace." MODERN AFFIRMATION

70 **Real blessings** "Our real blessings often appear to us in the shapes of pains, losses and disappointments; but let us have patience, and we soon shall see them in their proper figures."
Joseph Addison (1672–1719)

71 **Your guardian angel** People of many religions report encounters with angels – mystical beings who rescue them from danger. This meditation introduces you to your angel so that you can call on him or her in times of need. First light a candle to welcome the light of your angel into your life. Sit before the candle with your hands in your lap, palms upward – this position indicates your willingness to accept divine intervention in your life. Close your eyes and take a few deep breaths to relax your body. As you sit there become aware of a presence behind you, exuding warmth and comfort. Feel yourself embraced by the presence. Draw strength from the sense of security this brings you.

How to behave

POSITIVE PERSPECTIVES

72   **Think positive** Meditation helps us to develop the capacity
         to observe our thoughts from a neutral place rather than
         identifying with them. This enables us to watch the patterns
         of our thinking on a constant basis. When you notice negative
         thoughts arising, observe them without judgment before
         replacing them with more positive thoughts.

73   **The mudfish** "Live like a mudfish, whose stain is bright and
         silvery even though it dwells in mud." RAMAKRISHNA (1836–86)

74   **The energizing shower** Close your eyes and imagine
         cleansing spring water pouring into you through the crown
         of your head, deep into your being and then out through your
         feet. The water brings positive ions, charged with the spirit of
         "can", that replace all the negative "can't" ions. By the end of
         the meditation, you feel refreshed and primed for positive action.

75   **Affirmations** An affirmation is a simple, positive "I am ..."
         statement, such as "I am a compassionate being of light", that

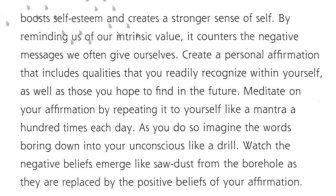

boosts self-esteem and creates a stronger sense of self. By reminding us of our intrinsic value, it counters the negative messages we often give ourselves. Create a personal affirmation that includes qualities that you readily recognize within yourself, as well as those you hope to find in the future. Meditate on your affirmation by repeating it to yourself like a mantra a hundred times each day. As you do so imagine the words boring down into your unconscious like a drill. Watch the negative beliefs emerge like saw-dust from the borehole as they are replaced by the positive beliefs of your affirmation.

76 **Brighter prospects** "A single gentle rain makes the grass many shades greener. So our prospects brighten on the influx of better thoughts." HENRY DAVID THOREAU (1817–62)

77 **Make it less personal** A tendency to take all irritations as personal insults can indicate an underlying lack of self-belief. If you catch yourself making paranoid assumptions, spend some time questioning their logic. Is the builder hammering outside really making a noise just to annoy you or is he simply doing his job? When we cease to take irritations personally, we may still find them unpleasant but we no longer react so emotively.

78 **The problem balloon** "I refuse to let my problems swell up inside me like a balloon and disfigure my self-image. I am dealing with them. The balloon is shrivelling. I can still function as my whole self." MODERN AFFIRMATION

79 **Raindrops** "The raindrops patter on the basho leaf; but these are not tears of grief; this is only the anguish of him who is listening to them." EASTERN SAYING

80 **Perseus's shield** In the face of intractable problems, feelings of paralysis can sometimes set in. The story of the Greek hero Perseus offers a way to overcome such feelings. Perseus's problem is represented by the snake-haired gorgon Medusa, whose face turns to stone those who look upon it directly. Perseus manages to slay Medusa by observing her in the

reflection of his shield. We can approach our own problems
in a similar way, viewing them obliquely rather than head on.

81   **Beautiful things** "I never saw an ugly thing in my life: for let
the form of an object be what it may – perspective, light and
shade will always make it beautiful." JOHN CONSTABLE (1776–1837)

82   **A global perspective** Considering problems within a larger
context can render them easier to bear. Imagine orbiting the
Earth in a space rocket. Satellites beam images to your console
from around the world: farmers harvesting grain in Canada;
city-workers streaming through the streets of Tokyo; elephants
trekking across the plains of Africa. As you watch these activities,
your anxieties diminish, seeming insignificant on a global scale.

83   **Soar like a bird** This will give you a higher viewpoint on a
difficult situation. Imagine that your arms have transformed into
a pair of wings. You flap your wings and take off, soaring into
the air. Looking down at your problem, you see it in a whole

new light. Set against a vast panorama, it appears far smaller and less significant than before. You can also see other aspects of the problem that you were previously blind to – other people's roles, different viewpoints, the causes of the situation, even solutions. With the benefit of these new insights, you return to Earth, ready to face your problem afresh.

84 **Shift perspective** Changing perspectives on a situation can help you to resolve the difficulties it presents. First visualize the situation in your mind in full detail. Then shift your perspective by bringing the background to the foreground and vice versa. How does this alter your understanding of the situation?

Alternatively, imagine the situation in a **different light (85)**, from a **different angle (86)** or from the **other person's viewpoint (87)**.

88 **Planting happiness** Every thought that we have, every image that we create, is a seed of our future reality. To be happy we must see ourselves as happy. First hold in your mind the idea of happiness – ask yourself what it means to you on a mental, emotional and spiritual level. Now imagine yourself being happy from inside out. What does it feel like? How do you behave? How do others respond to you? Having rehearsed this state of happiness in your mind, embody it throughout the day in all your thoughts, feelings and actions.

Adapt this exercise to suit any state or quality that you would like to manifest in your life, such as **peace (89)** or **love (90)**.

91 **Brahma's example** Brahma is the Creator God – one of the triad of gods at the heart of Hindu mythology. It is believed that Brahma created the world by meditating. Contemplate your own world as it is now. How do your current thoughts create your reality? Now meditate on your life as you would like it to be.

92 **Follow your dreams** "Go confidently in the direction of your dreams! Live the life you've imagined. As you simplify your life, the laws of the universe will be simpler." HENRY DAVID THOREAU (1817–62)

93 **Blind Justice** When bad things happen to us, there is a temptation to look for someone to blame – whether ourselves or another person. As an antidote meditate on the image of Blind Justice. With her scales, sword and blindfold, she reminds us that, from a broader spiritual perspective, reality is always just – everything happens for a reason, although at the time we may not understand what the reason is. From this perspective it becomes easier to accept events as they are.

94 **Adaptation** "A wise man adapts himself to circumstances, as water shapes itself to the vessel that contains it." CHINESE PROVERB

95 **Reconciliation with gravity** Those who feel anxious in the face of insuperable obstacles often owe their anxiety to the suspicion that the obstacles are not truly insuperable, and that finding them so reflects badly upon their capabilities. Such people expend energy on finding a way that may not exist and feeling bad about failure. You cannot will yourself into the sky, so don't even attempt it.

96   **Accepting what is** "Learn to wish that everything should come to pass exactly as it does." EPICTETUS (55–c.135)

97   **Leaf lines** Contemplate the delicate veins fanning out from the stem of a leaf. They provide an image for the many paths a life can take. Use this image to reflect on your own life, tracing your way back to your stem. Notice how every choice you have made has played a part in bringing you to where you are now. This will help you to accept that every experience has taught you something new and moved you further along in your journey.

98   **Your Achilles' heel** As humans we all possess weaknesses, however strong we feel ourselves to be. A failure to take account of our limitations can have serious consequences. This was demonstrated by Achilles, the "invincible" Trojan hero, who died when pierced by an arrow in his ankle – his one weak point.

Contemplate your own Achilles' heel. What feelings do your weaknesses evoke in you? As you observe your feelings, see if you can begin to accept your weaknesses.

99   **A settled mind** "The mind becomes settled when it cultivates friendliness in the face of happiness, compassion in the face of misery, joy in the face of virtue, and indifference in the face of error." PATANJALI (2ND CENTURY BCE)

100   **Following the cart** As human beings our predicament is like that of a dog leashed to an unpredictable cart: reality grants us a certain amount of free rein but prevents us from wandering where we please. When we struggle against events over which we have no control, our suffering increases. In such instances the only wise option is to resign ourselves to fate.

101   **First and last steps** "One's first step in wisdom is to question everything – and one's last is to come to terms with everything." GEORG CHRISTOPH LICHTENBERG (1742–99)

HUMILITY

102 **A prayer for humility** Humility involves acknowledging
our place as part of a greater whole. To enhance your awareness
of this, close your eyes and spend a minute or two in prayer,
asking to be opened to the presence of the universal spirit.

As a variation adopt **a humble position (103)** as you pray,
kneeling with head bowed and hands clasped in front of you.

104 **The heavenly lights** "Humility like darkness reveals the
heavenly lights." HENRY DAVID THOREAU (1817–62)

105 **Coronations** "People who are perfect leave no trace of their
actions," says the Taoist philosopher Chuang Tzu. All virtues are
crowned by their own humility.

106 **The line at the well** Consider your needs. Now, as an
exercise in humility, imagine that everyone in the world is
allotted a place in a line leading to a magic well that can
satisfy everyone's needs. Your place is at the tail-end of the line.
From here you can view all the worthier people ahead of you. In

each step forward you take great pleasure because the worthiest person at the front of the line can now take their healing draft.

107   **Concealing good** "I will conceal the good that I have done to others, while advertising the good that others have done to me." ALI, FIRST IMAN OF THE SHI'A BRANCH OF ISLAM (C.600–661)

108   **Night-sky meditation** A clear starry night offers the perfect opportunity for a night-sky meditation. Lie down on your back outside so that you can observe the sky in comfort. As you gaze up at the dark expanse above you, open your heart to the immensities of the cosmos. Experience humility in the face of something so beautiful, mysterious and all-encompassing. Our lives are but the blinks of an eye in the life-span of the universe.

109   **Perfect faith** "That man is perfect in faith who can come to God in the utter dearth of his feelings and desires, without a glow or aspiration, with the weight of low thoughts, and say to him: 'You are my refuge.'" GEORGE MACDONALD (1824–1905)

MOTIVATIONS AND DESIRES

110   **The choice** "I turn my attention inward to sense the tug of hidden desires. Clear in my self-awareness, I am now free to make my choice." MODERN AFFIRMATION

111   **Acting from the Self** "Get rid of the self and act from the Self!" ZEN SAYING

112   **Seas of hidden motivation** There are times when we feel driven by forces that we don't understand. This visualization helps bring awareness to these unconscious motivations. Imagine that you are a deep-sea diver, plunging into the depths of the sea. Out of the gloom looms the dark form of a ship-wreck. You swim into the wreck through a porthole. In one corner you see the glint of a brass key in the lock of a wooden chest. You turn the key to open the chest. What lies inside? What does this tell you about the impulses that drive you?

113   **Becoming what we worship** "A person will worship something, have no doubt about that. We may think our tribute is paid in secret in the dark recesses of our hearts, but it will out. That which dominates our imaginations and our thoughts will determine our lives, and our character. Therefore, it behoves us to be careful what we worship, for what we are worshiping we are becoming." RALPH WALDO EMERSON (1803–1882)

114 **Speak for your passions** Passion is wholehearted enthusiasm: a feeling for whatever is indispensable in the world and in your life. Ask yourself what passions you have – perhaps a commitment to your local community or a feeling for nature. Imagine being asked to sacrifice various comforts for the sake of one of these passions. You do so, whereupon a ceremony of thanksgiving is held in your honour. Compose the speech you would make on such an occasion – making sure that you express due gratitude for whatever your passion has brought you (the opportunity to serve your town, the bounty of nature).

115 **Stoke the inner fire** Just behind the navel lies the yellow *manipura chakra*. (The *chakras* are the main energy centres of the body. There are seven in total.) The *manipura chakra* connects us with the energy of the sun and is associated with the fire element. It is the source of willpower, providing us with the impetus for all our actions. Meditating on the *manipura chakra* helps to boost willpower and motivation. To do this, visualize a yellow sphere spinning behind your navel. If you find it difficult to visualize the sphere in motion, it may be that your *manipura chakra* is blocked. Place both hands, one on top of the other, over your navel and continue the visualization. This should help to unblock the energy, allowing the sphere to spin once more.

116 The significance of our longing "The significance of a man is not in what he attains but rather in what he longs to attain." KAHLIL GIBRAN (1883–1931)

117 Focus on a pebble You can use a pebble as a talisman to act as a focus for your ambitions and goals. Hold the pebble in your hand and focus your attention on it. Look at the smooth grain of its surface and the variations in hue, and feel the cool hardness of the pebble against your skin. Now close your eyes and, squeezing the pebble tightly in one hand, wish for the fulfilment of an important dream or goal. As you do so imagine that the stone is glowing in your hand, charged with the energy of your wish. Put the stone in a place where you will see it on a daily basis to remind you of your goal.

Whenever you are about to take a step toward achieving your goal and require an extra boost, squeeze the stone in your hand to summon your energies and focus your mind.

As well as pebbles, there are many other things that you can use as talismans – for example, a **semi-precious stone or crystal (118)**, a **pendant (119)** or a small **toy or doll (120)**.

121 **Goals that matter** "I can achieve any goal I set myself if I choose my goals wisely. I dedicate myself to the goals that really matter." MODERN AFFIRMATION

122 Aim above the mark "If you would hit the mark, you must aim a little above it;/ Every arrow that flies feels the attraction of earth." HENRY WADSWORTH LONGFELLOW (1807–1882)

123 Hitting the target Zen master Chuang Tzu asserted that the need to win can drain an archer of his power. By focusing on what we are doing, we can be both mindful and spontaneous. This frees us from any thoughts of winning or losing, and allows us to execute our will clearly and effectively. Try to draw your bow without being attached to the outcome. Whether or not you hit the target will be determined by how successful you are in freeing yourself from this burden of anxiety.

124 The edge of the forest "On the edge of the forest live joyfully, without desire." THE BUDDHA (c.563–c.460BCE)

125 Saturn versus Jupiter In astrological terms Saturn is the planet of restraint, responsibility, limitation and self-discipline, while Jupiter is the planet of expansion, growth, spontaneity and creativity. A balance of both influences is necessary in our lives: too much Saturn and we fail to achieve our full creative potential; too much Jupiter and we over-extend ourselves, becoming irresponsible in our ambitions. Meditate on the planet whose influence you feel you lack, visualizing either the cold, grey sphere of seven-ringed Saturn, or the red giant of Jupiter.

126 Limits "There are limits to self-indulgence, none to self-restraint." MAHATMA GANDHI (1869–1948)

127 Imperfections "I do not seek perfection – only to do the best that I can. If others do better, I will admire them without envy while trying to do better myself." MODERN AFFIRMATION

128 The superiority complex Those who believe themselves greater than others secretly fear themselves less.

129 **The flight of Icarus** According to Greek mythology, Icarus was a young man who tried to escape from a labyrinth wearing a pair of waxen wings made by his father Daedalus. However, despite his father's warnings, Icarus flew too close to the sun, his wings melted and he fell to the Earth. Hold this story in your mind to remind yourself of the need to balance idealism and aspiration with a realistic awareness of human limitation.

130 **Greed** "There is no greater disaster than greed."
LAO TZU (c.604–531BCE)

131 **An end to grasping** "How shall I grasp it? Do not grasp it. That which remains when there is no more grasping is the Self."
SWAMI VIDYARANYA (c.1268–c.1386)

132 **Releasing attachments** Think of an attachment you would like to be rid of – perhaps to something that addicts you, such as chocolate, or overdependence on a friend or relative. Visualize yourself walking across a landscape toward a distant castle – the place you want to be. Tied to your waist is a rope, which trails behind you and slows your progress; at the other end of the rope is a box, containing the essence of your attachment. The box is heavy and slows you down. You take out a knife and cut the rope: this is your decision to control the habit. As you make the cut, consider the action to be a turning point. Your journey will be much easier without this burden.

133 **Two golden birds** Imagine two golden birds perched in a tree. The first bird eats the sweet and sour fruits of the tree, while the second looks on without eating. Thinking that we are the first bird – the ego – we feel attached and fall into sorrow; realizing that we are the second bird – the Self – we are freed from sorrow, for the Self is the source of all light and love. ADAPTED FROM THE *BHAGAVAD GITA* (1ST OR 2ND CENTURY)

134 **The reality of detachment**
"Attachment is the great fabricator of illusions; reality can be attained only by someone who is detached." SIMONE WEIL (1909–1943)

135 Clearing out the attic Imagine yourself in the attic of your psyche. Around you are piles of boxes filled with your attachments. One by one you remove each box from the attic and empty it out with the garbage. As you do so a sense of lightness steals over you. At last you are free.

136 Victory over the self "I count him braver who overcomes his desires than him who conquers his enemies; for the hardest victory is over the self." ARISTOTLE (384–322BCE)

137 A vivid world We all develop addictions. When we gain mastery over them, our experience of the world is enriched. We thought we were seeing the rainbow. We weren't. We were seeing in black-and-white. Only now, addiction-free, do we see the world in all its glory.

138 The means and the end "Meditation is not the means to an end. It is both the means and the end." JIDDU KRISHNAMURTI (1895–1986)

CHOICE AND RESPONSIBILITY

139 **Quilting** Creating a life is like making a patchwork quilt: you have to choose your combinations carefully. The right choices will enhance your quilt. The wrong choices will dull the fabrics and hide their original beauty. You have to trust your instinct and you have to be bold.

140 **Self-rule** "No one outside myself can rule me inwardly. Knowing this I become wholly free." MODERN AFFIRMATION

141 **Breaking free** When we cease to be ourselves it is because at some point in our lives unsuitable controls have been placed on our outward behaviour. However, in our thoughts we can free ourselves from this bondage. Recognize in your mind that you are free. Break the ties and rejoice in the freedom of the spirit.

142 **Secret words** "I have given you words of vision and wisdom more secret than hidden mysteries. Ponder them in the silence of your soul, and then in freedom do your will." BHAGAVAD GITA (1ST OR 2ND CENTURY)

143 Free will "I am no bird, and no net ensnares me: I am a free human being with an independent will." JANE EYRE, IN THE NOVEL BY CHARLOTTE BRONTË (1847)

144 Living consciously "Every moment lived consciously is a step toward spiritual maturity. I offer my experience as an example for others making the journey." MODERN AFFIRMATION

145 From another world "Our freedom is but a light that breaks through from another world." NIKOLAI GUMILEV (1886–1921)

146 To the lighthouse "I am lighthouse rather than lifeboat. I do not rescue, but instead help others to find their own way to shore, guiding them by my example." MODERN AFFIRMATION

147 A game of chess When faced with difficult choices, view the situation as if

it were a game of chess. Imagine those involved as pieces on the chess-board. Assume the role of one of the players and meditate on the current state of play. From this position the dynamics of the situation may become clearer, enabling you to see the options open to you and to make a wiser choice.

148 **The snowflake** "No snowflake in an avalanche ever feels responsible." VOLTAIRE (1694–1778)

149 **Taming wild horses** At times we may feel that our desires are completely out of control. To regain self-possession visualize these desires as a group of wild horses dragging behind them a chariot of which you are the rider. Firmly but gently begin to tighten the reins and, as you do so, feel the horses slow down, responding as you regain self-control.

150 **Dressage** This is a disciplined form of horse-riding in which the horse responds sensitively to the rider's wishes. The object is to achieve harmony between horse and rider. Imagine yourself as a dressage rider: focused and present, you engage in seamless communication with your horse. Translate this into your relations with yourself. Be at one with yourself, fully aware and able to choose how you respond to the world in each moment.

151 **Destiny's harvest** "Sow an act, and you reap a habit. Sow a habit, and you reap a character. Sow a character, and you reap a destiny." CHARLES READE (1814–84)

152 **The human condition** According to the sixteenth-century French philosopher Michel de Montaigne, each one of us carries the full burden of the human condition. All that we see in others – both the darkness and the light – is also present in ourselves.

153 **The call of the heart** "Everyone should carefully observe which way his heart draws him, and then choose that way with all his strength." HASIDIC SAYING

RIGHT ACTION

154 The executives of virtue All virtues increase each other's powers. Kindness is empowered by courage and courage by kindness. Patience is empowered by strength and strength by patience. All virtues are executive powers of love and peace.

155 An army of goodness Goodness is the captain, good deeds the soldiers. ADAPTED FROM LEONARDO DA VINCI (1452–1519)

156 Aim above morality "Do not be too moral. You may cheat yourself out of so much of life. So aim above morality. Be not simply good; be good for something." HENRY DAVID THOREAU (1817–62)

157 Glistening jewels Human virtues, like glistening jewels, or beauty itself, ask for nothing in return for what they give. ADAPTED FROM MARCUS AURELIUS (121–180)

158 Virtue by stealth "Do good by stealth, and blush to find it fame." ALEXANDER POPE (1688–1744)

159 **A juggling act** "I juggle the demands of my life with grace, catching balls that give me purpose and putting down, without guilt or anxiety, those that drain my energy."
MODERN AFFIRMATION

160 **Polishing virtues** Imagine that you are handling a wooden bowl, polished with the patina of age. Every time you handle it you are adding to its lovely polish. Pick a noble quality and imagine it gaining sheen in the same way, becoming more brilliant every time someone touches it. Make your own contribution to its shine.

161 **Creating wealth** "Energy creates energy. It is by spending oneself that one becomes rich." SARAH BERNHARDT (1844–1923)

162 **The scent of goodness** When we try all the time to be good, a spiritual beauty steals into our hearts, like the scent of wild flowers hidden among the grass.

163 **The shadow of happiness** "I resolve to speak and act with a pure mind. When I do, happiness follows as my shadow." MODERN AFFIRMATION

164 **Ordinary lives** Do not assume that only those lives marked by grand achievements or spectacular heroics have value. An ordinary life, striving for virtue and wisdom, is an achievement in itself.

165 **Giving oneself** "To give of one's self; to leave the world a bit better, whether by a healthy child, a garden patch, or a redeemed social condition ... to know that even one life has

breathed easier because you have lived – this is to have
succeeded." RALPH WALDO EMERSON (1803–1882)

166 **Karmic laws** Within many wisdom paths is the belief that life
is governed by karma – the spiritual law of cause and effect.
This law states that our actions in this life dictate the rewards
we will receive in the next. Close your eyes and spend a few
minutes considering how your actions impact on your own life
and the lives of those around you. How would your life differ
if you strived to be kind, generous and thoughtful at all times?
Good karma depends upon pure intentions, so it is important to
try to release any thoughts of self-gain as a result of your good
actions. Resolve that from now on you will make an effort to
respond to all situations, whether easy or difficult, with
consideration for others and generosity of spirit.

167 **Doing a little** "Nobody made a greater mistake than he who
did nothing because he could only do a little." EDMUND BURKE
(1729–97)

168 **A challenge for virtue** Just as medicine is pointless unless it drives away our illness or our pain, so too virtue is useless unless we exercise it in situations where it is challenged.

169 **Stepping stones** "Every charitable act is a stepping stone toward heaven." HENRY WARD BEECHER (1813–87)

170 **Cleansing the self** Whenever you feel that you have done something wrong, phrase to yourself a simple statement of what

you have done, followed by a declaration of what was wrong
with it, followed by an avowal of remedial action in the future.
Say these sentences over to yourself six times. Let their full
import sink in. Afterwards, remember, but do not become
obsessed by, your mistake; and be true to your avowal.

171   **Purifying fire**   May my own actions burn off my rusts and my
deformity. ADAPTED FROM JOHN DONNE (1572–1631)

172   **The conch shell**   In India the conch shell is an auspicious
symbol, representing the power of Hindu teachings. Visualize
the spirals of the conch – denoting the beauty of true belief.
Imagine putting the conch to your ear and hearing the sounds
of the sea – denoting the depth of true wisdom. Picture yourself
blowing on the conch like a trumpet – denoting the values you
will demonstrate to the world by your speech and your actions.

173   **Prepare and maintain**   "What is well-planted will not be torn
up. What is well-kept will not escape." LAO TZU (C.604–531BCE)

174 **Fireflies** Be not consumed by the darkness that surrounds you, but let your virtues shine forth – a host of fireflies, dancing and glowing in the night.

175 **The toils of Hercules** According to Greek myth, Hercules reveals his true heroism by undertaking twelve gruelling tasks in penance for his errors. In one such task he slays the Lernaean Hydra – a nine-headed water snake. Reflect on the myth of Hercules to give you the strength to choose virtue, even when it entails the most challenging struggles.

176 **The time is ripe** "We must use time creatively, and forever realize that the time is always ripe to do right." MARTIN LUTHER KING, JR. (1929–68)

177 **The path of fire** The Chinese philosopher Confucius tells us that "To see what is right and not to do it is want of courage." So walk bravely on the path of fire. Take action where action is called for, even at the risk of burning your feet.

178 **Seeing the obvious** Peace comes not from disengagement with the world but from seeing what needs to be done and acting in the light of that perception.

179 **Speaking your truth** The Greek philosopher Socrates spent his life using rational logic to challenge the norms of his society. Even with his life at stake, he refused to conform, determined to uphold what he knew to be true. Approach your own life with a similar attitude. Probe beneath the surface of supposed "truths" presented to you by others as you search for your own truth.

180 **Mountains and jewelry** When we are climbing mountains, we do not seek the judgment of jewellers. When we are making jewelry, we do not seek the judgment of mountaineers.

181 **Crisis management** When a crisis looms, summon up a close friend in your imagination. Imagine his or her calming words of support. As you enter the fray, you know they're on your side, influencing for the better every move you make.

Finding
your strengths

COURAGE

182 **True courage** According to Socrates courage is not a display of brute strength but endurance or action combined with a moral sense – in other words, intelligent endurance or action. Bearing in mind this definition, consider the times in your life when you have displayed courage. As you recall those experiences, resolve to bring this attitude to the challenges that you are currently facing or expect to face in the future.

183 **Daniel in the lion's den** In the Old Testament we are told of the courage of Daniel, a young man who survives a night in the lion's den, protected by the strength of his faith. Be inspired by Daniel's example. Have faith that if you do what is right, and have the courage to adhere to your values, ultimately all will be well for you.

184 **Finding the core of light** We often find ourselves complying with the will of others against our own wishes, because we fear the rejection that might result if we fail to

cooperate. However, in doing so we betray ourselves, thereby
further damaging our self-esteem. Whenever you feel subject
to such external pressures, close your eyes and visualize a core
of golden light running from your feet, through your body and
out through the top of your head. Experience the light as a
source of strength, radiating through every fibre of your being.

185   Expansion and contraction "Life shrinks or expands
in proportion to one's courage." ANAÏS NIN (1903–1977)

186 **The birth of Athene** Athene, one of the most powerful of the Greek goddesses, was born, fully armed, from the head of Zeus. On one level we can understand her as a representation of our inner warrior – embodiment of the innate strengths within each one of us. In your mind conjure an image of Athene, furnished with helmet, shield and spear. Focus on this image and draw courage from the strengths she represents in you.

187 **Fearlessness** "I have only to believe that I have no fear, and all my fear will melt away. I have only to believe in myself, and all my obstacles will lose their threat." MODERN AFFIRMATION

188 **Releasing fear** If we allow them their way, our fears can exert a powerful influence over our thoughts, feelings and actions. Perform this meditation to loosen their grip. **1** Close your eyes and bring to mind one of your deepest fears – for example, the fear of being unlovable. **2** Acknowledge the presence of your fear. Just be aware of its existence and observe how it feels without wallowing in it. **3** Now imagine your fear embodied as a caged bird. Notice the appearance of the bird – its shape, the colour of its feathers, the sound of its call, and its movements. **4** Visualize opening the cage and setting the bird free, releasing it from your consciousness. As you watch the bird fly away, experience a wave of acceptance washing over you.

189 **The call of the drum** There are times when simply continuing with life is an achievement. To have the strength to keep going at such times, listen to and draw courage from the inner drum of your heartbeat. Hear its rhythm of purposeful determination – it is the call to life itself.

190 **Ride on singing** "If you have a fearful thought, do not share it with someone who is weak: whisper it to your saddle-bow, and ride on singing." KING ALFRED OF WESSEX (849–899)

191 **Dissolving fear** Our fear is of the unknown. Let go, throw yourself into the adventure of the self. The fear fades into the air you breathe.

192   **Daring to act**   "It is not because things are difficult that we do not dare; it is because we do not dare that they are difficult." SENECA (C.4BCE–65CE)

193   **The sphinx**   A mythical creature, the sphinx combines the forms of a human, lion, eagle and bull. Ancient Egyptians  placed statues of sphinxes outside sacred places to provide protection. Visualize a sphinx made up of four animals whose traits you would find helpful in your life. Bring your sphinx to mind whenever you need protection.

194   **Blue auras**   In challenging situations, imagine that you are completely surrounded by an envelope of blue light. This will help to prevent your energy from being leached by those around you, as blue is associated with protection and tranquillity. Imagine negative energies bouncing off your aura. Feel safe in the knowledge that nothing can truly harm you.

195 **Moving through darkness** During times of darkness in our lives, we often feel lost and afraid. To find a way through these feelings, imagine that you are running through a dark forest. You pause and take several deep breaths. As you do so you notice a clearing ahead. You enter the clearing and rest there for a moment. Then you spot a path leading out of the clearing. You follow the path until finally you emerge into the sunlight.

196 **Finding the gift** Characteristic of depression is a feeling of entrapment in a meaningless void. Trips into this psychic underworld are scary, yet there can be surprising benefits for those brave enough to confront the darkness. If you find yourself in such a place, imagine walking down a long, dark tunnel. When you feel you can go no further, a faceless figure looms out of the shadows. He places the bud of a white rose in your hands before slipping away into the darkness. Continuing along the tunnel you spy light ahead. As you emerge into the sunlight, the rose bursts into bloom: it is the flowering of wisdom and insight, gained from your journey into yourself.

FORTITUDE

197   **Grounding yourself** **1** Sit comfortably and close your eyes.
2 Focus your attention on the *muladhara* (root) *chakra* at the base
of your spine. **3** During each inhalation, imagine that you are
drawing strength from the ground up into your spine and the
rest of your body. **4** During each exhalation, sense your strength
increasing. Throughout, try to maintain an awareness of the
connection between the base of your body and the ground.

198   **Breath of the dawn** "Take the breath of the new dawn
and make it part of you. It will give you strength." HOPI SAYING

199   **Sources of strength** "The universe is an endless source
of strength I can draw on as I undertake new challenges."
MODERN AFFIRMATION

200   **Into the canyon** Imagine yourself walking across a vast
plateau of barren, red rock. Suddenly you find yourself at the
edge of a canyon. You follow a path down the steep walls of the
canyon. As you descend the air dampens and lush greenery

envelops you. When you reach the river at the bottom of
the canyon, you wade into shallows and immerse yourself in
the water. As you do so a sense of power courses through your
body – this river is the source of your inner strength, running
deeper than you had ever imagined. Repeat this journey into
the canyon whenever you need to contact your inner strength.

201 **Listen for the bells** According to myth Celtic shamans used
sacred branches hung with silver bells to open doors between
the material and spirit worlds. Close your eyes and imagine
hearing the music of the silver bells. Approaching the sound
you see a gateway formed by two blossoming trees. Passing
through, you find yourself in another world. Ahead of you
the guardian of the gateway is tending a cauldron over a fire.
The guardian fills a chalice with liquid from the cauldron and
hands it to you. The spicy drink replenishes your strength. The
guardian tells you to return whenever you need to, reminding
you to listen for the silver bells. You pass back through the
gateway and open your eyes. You feel full of life and energy.

202 A prayer for strength
"O Lord, I do not pray for tasks equal to my strength: I ask for strength equal to my tasks." PHILLIPS BROOKS (1835–93)

203 The well of experience
Our inner resources are bottomless – like the spirit itself. Next time you need to draw upon some aspect of your inner strength – perhaps your courage, patience or tolerance – imagine lowering a bucket into a well. No matter how much energy you draw from this source, there will

always be vast reserves still left in place. As you raise your bucket, make a vow to use this energy wisely and lovingly.

204   **Bearing troubles** "Nothing happens to any man that he is not formed by nature to bear." MARCUS AURELIUS (121–180)

205   **Clay and iron** "Mould clay and submit to iron." MODERN MEDITATION FROM CHINA

206   **The full moon** According to Pagan belief the full moon is a time for garnering strengths and committing to new ventures. To help you do this, meditate on the full moon. Allow the luminous white disk to fill your consciousness. Imagine the white light flooding your being with strength and energy.

207   **Your personal totem** Like coats of arms Native American totem poles depict symbols representing the qualities with which all members of a community identify. They therefore serve as a source of strength and unity. To create a personal totem, choose symbols to represent your personality and ties of allegiance to family and friends. Draw these symbols and attach the drawings to a wooden stick. Meditate on your miniature totem pole to remind you of your individual and collective identity.

Alternatively, depict the symbols in a **collage (208)**, or **painting (209)** and meditate on this instead.

210 **The energy mudra** To gain a fresh perspective and a boost of confidence and energy, practise the *apan mudra* during meditation. (*Mudras* are positions – mostly of the hands – that affect the body's energetic system.) **1** Sit comfortably and rest your hands on your thighs, palms facing up. **2** On each hand bring the tips of your middle and ring fingers to touch the tip of your thumb. **3** Allow your index and little fingers to extend softly forward. **4** With your eyes closed hold this *mudra* for five minutes, two to three times a day, or as you feel you need it.

211 **Be a tree** Visualize yourself as a tree with branches reaching to the sky and roots extending deep into the earth. As you

inhale imagine you are drawing air and sunlight down
through your branches into your trunk. As you exhale imagine
the breath continuing down through your roots and into the
earth. On the next inhalation, imagine bringing the energy of
the earth up through your roots into your trunk. Exhale out
through your branches. Continue breathing in alternate
directions like this for five to ten minutes.

212 **The self-relying soul** "The poise of a plant, the bended tree recovering itself from the strong wind, the vital resources of every vegetable and animal, are also demonstrations of the self-sufficing, and therefore self-relying soul. All history from its highest to its trivial passages is the various record of this power." RALPH WALDO EMERSON (1803–1882)

213 **In Noah's shadow** "In perfect faith I wait, surveying the troubled seas of my life for the gentle doves of hope." MODERN AFFIRMATION

214 **Building stamina** Practise this visualization to give you the strength to keep going when problems seem insurmountable. Visualize yourself at the bottom of a mountain whose summit is enshrouded in cloud. You embark on the long and arduous ascent – the path is steep and rocky, the damp air chills your skin and the mist grows ever thicker. You concentrate on putting one foot in front of the other, trusting that the path will deliver you to your destination. Near the summit the clouds disperse and the way ahead becomes clear. You realize that as long as you have the strength to keep going, all challenges are conquerable.

215 **The storm within** "The wise man in the storm prays to God, not for safety from danger, but for deliverance from fear. It is the storm within that endangers him, not the storm without." RALPH WALDO EMERSON (1803–1882)

216 **Rejoice in achievement** As well as feeling proud of your own achievements, you can derive a great deal of pleasure from the achievements of others, whether those of friends, family, acquaintances or even people you don't know. Consider some of the achievements of other people that you have heard about recently. What can you learn from these successes? Seek to draw strength, courage and motivation from these examples to enable you to work toward your own goals.

SELF-AWARENESS

217   True image "Lack of self-respect warps the mirror: I will walk away from this distorted image of myself before the illusion becomes part of my landscape. I am whole and unique."
MODERN AFFIRMATION

218   The characteristics of excellence "Not to be cheered by praise, not to be grieved by blame, but to know thoroughly one's own virtues or powers, are the characteristics of excellence." SASKYA PANDITA (1182–1252)

219   Questioning the self Who am I? When meditating, observe your thoughts as they drift across your mind. Do not engage with them: just let them happen. Ask yourself, who is it who is watching these thoughts? Ask lightly, without expecting any enlightenment. One day you will realize that deep in your heart you know the answer.

220   By lamplight "You must be lamps unto yourselves."
THE BUDDHA (C.563–C.460BCE)

221   **Behind the masks** Throughout our lives we perform various
social roles. If we're not careful, we can find ourselves identifying
too closely with a particular role, which then becomes limiting.
What are the roles you currently associate with? Visualize
yourself in each of these roles. What masks and manners do
you adopt? What lies behind these masks. Who are you really?

222 **Meet yourself for the first time** Close your eyes and imagine that you are attending a party. A friend comes over and introduces you to yourself. What are your first impressions of this person? Engage yourself in conversation. How does the relationship develop between you? From this neutral perspective consider the strengths and weaknesses that you see in yourself. Use this awareness as a basis for change.

223 **Pearl fishing** "Pearls do not lie on the seashore. If you desire one you must dive for it." EASTERN SAYING

224 **Dive into your unconscious** The sea provides a metaphor for the unconscious. Imagined journeys into the sea therefore teach us much about ourselves. Picture yourself in a boat on the ocean. What do you see when you look over the side of the boat into the water? Imagine yourself diving in. Swim slowly down through the water. Call out to the inhabitants of the deep – the unknown aspects of your being – asking them to introduce themselves and communicate with you. Listen to what they say. Now swim back up to the surface. Each time you repeat this meditation, plunge further into the ocean in order to deepen your experience of yourself.

225 Looking in wonder "People travel to wonder at the height of mountains, at the huge waves of the sea, at the long courses of rivers, at the vast compass of the ocean, at the circular motion of the stars, and they pass by themselves without wondering." ST AUGUSTINE (354–430)

226 Meditation images Sometimes while we are meditating certain images come to us unsolicited. To understand the significance of these images it can help to draw them. Keep paper and pencils at hand during your meditation so that you can commit the images to paper afterwards. As you draw an image, you may find that it takes on a life of its own. Additional details may suggest themselves and the resulting picture may differ from the one you set out to draw. Contemplate the final drawing. Allow its meanings to suggest themselves to you.

227 **Create a life tree** In many traditions the tree is used as a profound metaphor for life. By meditating on your own tree of life, you will develop a stronger sense of self. Begin by tracing your way back to the roots of who you are – to the influences of home, society, family, friends and acquaintances. Notice the marks on the tree trunk, the scars that you have acquired during the challenging process of growing up and finding your place in the world. Appreciate the fruits of the tree – the various achievements you are proud of. Nurture its buds, for these are your goals and dreams, which will one day shape your future.

228 **Self-respect** "Dignity comes not in possessing honours, but in the knowledge that we deserve them." ARISTOTLE (384–322BCE)

229 The house of the self Close your eyes and visualize the exterior of a house. In your mind enter the house and explore the interior from the basement to the attic. As you look around notice the the colours, style and overall atmosphere of each room. After examining each room thoroughly, open your eyes and draw what you have seen. Reflect on the meaning of your house as a metaphor for your self. What understanding of yourself can you glean from this exploratory visualization?

230 Self-knowledge "He who knows others is wise; he who knows himself is enlightened." Lao Tzu (c.604–531BCE)

231 Doorways of the mind The mind has doorways that we must open to fulfil our potential for personal growth. As you meditate imagine yourself opening a door that leads to a higher level of awareness, a brighter illumination. As you pull the door toward you, light floods in from around its edges. Visualize yourself walking into this brighter room. As you do so an inner truth dawns – perhaps the purity of the spirit, or your endless capacity for love.

232 **Self-realization** "Having realized his own self as the Self, a person becomes selfless." *UPANISHADS* (c.1000BCE)

233 **The truth about myself** "To be a good friend to myself I will, without harshness, see the truth about myself, no matter how difficult or beautiful this truth may be." MODERN AFFIRMATION

234 **Soul preservation** "To know what you prefer instead of humbly saying Amen to what the world tells you you ought to prefer, is to have kept your soul alive." ROBERT LOUIS STEVENSON (1850–94)

235 **Stepping out** "When I step out, the world assembles itself around me like my awareness of being who I am, like my belief in the Divine." MODERN MEDITATION FROM SWEDEN

236 **Empty the cup** A Western scholar once visited a Zen master and asked to receive teachings. The master invited the scholar to tea, then proceeded to pour a cup for him. He did not stop when the cup was full but continued pouring until the tea overflowed. His point was that if a seeker's mind is preoccupied, there is no room for wisdom. To gain in insight we must empty the cup of the mind, rather than pour precepts into it.

237 **Pools of wisdom** Identify the sources of wisdom in your life. Perhaps you have been inspired by a teacher, friend or relative, a book, or some past experience. Make regular contact with those sources – your personal pools of wisdom. Cherish the gifts that each of these pools has yielded to you.

238 **Milk of wisdom** "The milk of cows of any colour is white. The sages declare that the milk is wisdom, and that the cows are the sacred scriptures." *UPANISHADS* (C.1000BCE)

239 **Inner wisdom** We tend to believe that the sources of true wisdom lie with the great and the good. Yet however modest our lives are, we are all capable of arriving at profound insights. All that is required is the willingness to attend to our own experience and to regard ourselves as having the potential for a rich inner life. As the French philospher Michel de Montaigne once said: "We are richer than we think, each one of us."

240 **Travel light** The Buddha said that on life's journey some gather wisdom, some gather stones and some gather nothing.

To gather wisdom you must follow your own path. If you rely solely on wise teachers, their wisdom may weigh you down, like stones in your pockets, and impede your way.

241 **Wisdom within** "Compose yourself in stillness, draw your attention inward and devote your mind to the Self. The wisdom you seek lies within." *BHAGAVAD GITA* (1ST OR 2ND CENTURY)

242 **Not knowing** "To know yet to think that one does not know is best. Not to know yet to think that one knows will lead to difficulty." LAO TZU (C.604–531BCE)

243 **Inner lantern** Other people, even those we love and admire, sometimes question the path we choose. However, we should not let this be an obstacle, because our intuition will guide us. Venture bravely: your inner lantern will always light the way.

244 **Inside, outside** "Outside the room gain knowledge; inside the room gain wisdom." CHUANG TZU (C.369–286BCE)

245 **Look close** "Through what is near, one understands what is far away." HsüN Tzu (c.300–c.230BCE)

246 **Animal instincts** Greek mythology tells of a fabulous race of creatures called centaurs. Half-man, half-horse, a centaur reminds us of our intuitive nature, often repressed by the forces of civilization. Make contact with your own intuitive wisdom by turning your focus inward and bringing to mind an animal. What animal appears to you? Make friends with it and give it a name. You can now call on it to guide you whenever you are feeling lost or afraid.

247 **The Seer** The Celtic tradition tells of a figure called the Seer, who stands at the heart of the inner, personal universe, and is depicted as a beautiful female figure dressed in an owl's cloak – the symbol of her wisdom. Consult the Seer when you require assistance with personal issues, such as relationship problems. Imagine yourself in a moonlit glade. Before you is the Seer. Tell her what the problem is and ask for her advice. Listen carefully to her response, allowing her wisdom to seep into your mind. Know that you can return at any time to ask for her aid.

248   **Day dreaming** "Those who dream by day are cognizant of many things which escape those who dream only by night." EDGAR ALLAN POE (1809–1849)

249   **Wisdom of the ages** The figure of the Wise Old Man is a Jungian archetype. A source of ancient spiritual wisdom, this figure can take us to higher levels of consciousness, giving us new perspectives on our lives. To contact this archetype imagine yourself walking along a path through a dark forest. Suddenly you break through the trees and see the rocky summit of a mountain towering above you. Continuing up the path for some time, you see an old man sitting at the mouth of a cave. Approach the man with respect and introduce yourself. Describe the situation you are facing and ask for advice. What is his response? It may take the form of words, actions or images. How does his response shed light on your current predicament?

250 **The wisdom of silence** Think of yourself in a quiet place – perhaps a secluded room or a forest clearing. You are sitting in a chair or on a log. You try to speak words of wisdom but they die on your tongue. And with every word that dies, a pulse of beautiful energy flows back into your spirit. You feel wisdom building up inside you. You are learning the wisdom of silence. You stop trying to speak and you just sit there, becoming wiser and wiser with every moment.

251 **The still voice within** "The only tyrant I accept in this world is the still voice within." MAHATMA GANDHI (1869–1948)

252 **The heart of the spiral** Visualize yourself walking into a spiral maze of massive stones. Step by step you feel yourself becoming lighter, more connected to the spirit. In the quiet axis you feel in touch with your intuition. Do not break your meditation by asking any specific question: just remain silent and still, in the knowledge that all the wisdom you need lies deep inside you.

253 **Heart wisdom** "The heart that feels things deeply has wisdom. And wisdom as profound as that gives rise to virtue."
CHUANG TZU (C.369–286BCE)

254 **Tap your spiritual wisdom** The purple, "third eye" *chakra* (also called *ajna*, meaning "inner eye") is located in the middle of the forehead, just above the eyebrows. It is the centre for spiritual vision and rules our intellectual thought processes. Meditate on this energy centre by visualizing a purple sphere spinning in the middle of your forehead. This will

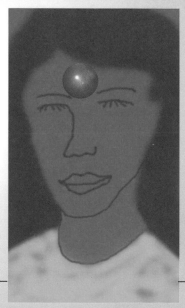

sharpen your mind and strengthen your connection to the
wisdom of the cosmos.

255 **First principles** "Hold faithfulness and sincerity as first
principles." CONFUCIUS (c.551–c.479BCE)

256 **The seal of wisdom** *Mudras* are positions (mostly of the
hands) that affect the body's energy system. The *jnana mudra* is
said to aid the direction of energy into the higher *chakras*,
lifting us into subtler states of consciousness. To perform this
mudra, sit comfortably and bring the tips of your index finger
and your thumb together on each hand. Rest your hands on
your knees, palms up. Closing your eyes, bring your attention
inward and observe any thoughts, feelings and sensations that
arise. Hold this *mudra* for between five and fifteen minutes.

257 **Knowing false and true** "The first point of wisdom is to
discern what is false; the second to know what is true."
LACTANTIUS (240–c.320)

CALM

258 **The omphalos** According to Greek mythology Zeus released two eagles from opposite ends of the Earth to discover the exact centre of the world. The eagles met at Delphi, and Zeus marked the spot with a large stone called an *omphalos*, meaning "navel". Meditate on your navel to strengthen your core. Sitting comfortably, place your fists together, with your elbows at right angles, and press gently on your navel. Now focus on your navel and breathe deeply, observing the movement of your fists.

259 **Rowing into meditation** Prepare for meditation by counting backward. Imagine rowing a boat toward a peaceful island. With each pull of the oars, feel your movements become more languid, your breathing slower, and your strokes longer and more relaxed. At the count of zero, you arrive on your island to begin your meditation.

260 **Follow the tortoise**
"Withdraw in meditation
from the pleasures of sense as a

tortoise withdraws its limbs. Through this will you find peace."
BHAGAVAD GITA (1ST OR 2ND CENTURY)

261 **Find your haven** When life gets stormy, feel safe in the
knowledge that the soul cannot be touched by external forces.
Like a ship finding shelter in a haven, take refuge in your soul
when things feel unsettled: it is the calm centre of your being.

262 **At rest** "I rest in tranquillity and divine grace. In this moment,
I am calm, happy and fulfilled." MODERN AFFIRMATION

263 **Find your reservoir of calm** At our core lies the peace of
our essential nature. To access this inner peace, visualize yourself
diving into the water of a warm, calm lake. You slip through the
water, surrounded by a profound silence. As you reach the
sea-bed, you are awed to see that it is carpeted with beautiful
white pearls. Imagine returning to the surface of the lake.
You realize that the silence, purity and beauty you have just
discovered lies within yourself.

264 **The lake of calm** Visualize a beautiful mountain lake, its surface smooth as glass. Feel a breeze come up, sending ripples across the water. Then, as the breeze dies, watch the ripples subside and the water become calm. Throughout the day, whenever a disturbance ruffles the surface of your mood, recall the image of the lake; feel the ripples of emotion settle into calm.

265 **The place of unity** "Away from the chatter of the senses, from the restless wanderings of the mind, there is a quiet pool of stillness. The wise call this stillness the highest state of being. It is the place where we find unity – never to become separate again."
UPANISHADS (C.1000BCE)

266 **Float in silence** In the modern world silence is a rare luxury. Yet it is important to give ourselves some silent time each day, because it is in moments of emptiness that spirit enters. A meditation on silence is best performed in a darkened room. Lie on the floor and focus on your breathing until your body feels completely relaxed. Now imagine that you're floating in the emptiness of space. Allow the silence to fill your body and mind. You become pure, floating awareness, at one with your surroundings.

267 **Inner peace** "Peace begins at home. When I come from a place of peace, I see peace around me." MODERN AFFIRMATION

268 **Steps to peace** "Keep the peace within yourself, then you can also bring peace to others." THOMAS À KEMPIS (c.1380–1471)

269 **Make peace** A peaceful heart is essential for well-being. The Vietnamese Zen monk Thich Nhat Hanh, a master of reconciliation, often speaks of being peace. As long as we feel the need to defend ourselves, the inner battle will continue. But when we can be peace – drop feelings of "us-versus-them" and live from a place that sees no separation from others – we can make peace with everyone, ourselves included.

270   **Dove of peace**   If you adopt the dove as your symbol of inner peace, you can summon it to come to your aid as a source of strength in times of difficulty. Consider what the dove symbolizes – love, compassion, truth. Nurture these qualities in yourself by meditating on the dove that resides within.

271   **Focus on inner stillness**   In the eye of a storm there is stillness. However chaotic, difficult or painful things appear, there remains a still point, an emptiness, at the core of your being where you can find peace. To find this place, close your eyes and turn your attention inward. Initially, observe the myriad pinpricks of flickering light that penetrate through your eyelids. Withdrawing deeper into yourself, the light recedes as you enter the vast space at the heart of your being – a place darker than darkness yet rich with potential, the sacred womb from which all things are born. It is here that you will find peace.

272   **God's stillness**   "Nothing in all creation is so like God as stillness." MEISTER ECKHART (c.1260–c.1327)

CREATIVITY

273   **Live authentically** In the words of Mahatma Gandhi, "Purity of life is the highest and truest art." If we can live authentically, in a way that is true to ourselves, this in itself is creative. All you need to do is accept and express who you are.

274   **True genius** "Genius means little more than the faculty of perceiving in an unhabitual way." WILLIAM JAMES (1842–1910)

275   **A singular voice in a choir of many** "I am a glorious, gifted creature, part of all creation yet unlike any other. I appreciate my special talents and singular voice." MODERN AFFIRMATION

276   **Live creatively** Creativity is our human expression of

the life-force, parallel to the daily miracles of nature, such as the transformation of caterpillars into butterflies and the blossoming of flowers. When we live creatively we align ourselves with the power behind these events. To do this we must surrender to a force greater than the ego, following the guidance of our hearts and trusting that our lives will unfold in the way that the universe intended.

277 **Paint your world** "The world is but a canvas to the imagination." HENRY DAVID THOREAU (1817–62)

278 **The Green Man** In the Celtic tradition the archetypal Father appears in several forms, one of which is the Green Man. Depicted with a wise, rugged face with hair and a beard of oak leaves, he is the defender of the land and the bestower of fertile energy. Call on the energy of the Green Man to help you become more creative and confident. Hold in mind the image of his face and ask for his assistance. Absorb his natural power and allow it to uplift you.

279 **Your special gifts** We all have gifts that we may not fully appreciate – unique talents that enrich our experiences and help us to face the challenges in our lives. Spend time reflecting on them. What personal qualities and creative talents do you have? Perhaps you are empathetic, funny or eloquent, a talented singer or a beautiful dancer. Acknowledge and cherish these unique gifts. Recognize them as blessings bequeathed to you for the benefit and enjoyment of yourself and others.

280 **Find your riches** "I have a wealth of knowledge and talents. Each day I spend some time in quiet contemplation to allow these riches to emerge." MODERN AFFIRMATION

281 **Hatch your gifts** In your mind's eye, visualize yourself as a bird perched beside a nest containing six identical eggs. Each egg contains a fledgling gift or talent that you possess. As you watch, one by one the eggs begin to hatch. As each chick breaks free from its shell, identify the gift it represents. As the parent bird your job is to feed and nurture your chicks to enable them to develop to their full potential. Imagine yourself providing this attention and watch the chicks grow from awkward, fragile little hatchlings into beautiful, fully-fledged birds. Now watch them take their first flights from the nest. As you do so acknowledge the potential of your gifts, and let them take wing.

282 **Immortal fruits** "Shun those studies whose fruits die with their maker." LEONARDO DA VINCI (1452–1519)

283 **My spiritual legacy** "My creativity is my spiritual legacy. I will use it to make gifts for myself and for everyone I care about." MODERN AFFIRMATION

284 **The waterfall of creativity** Surrender yourself to the creative flow of the universe. Rather than shivering on the rocks, plunge into the pool and allow the images to cascade over you.

285 **A channel for spirit** "I myself do nothing. The Holy Spirit accomplishes all through me." WILLIAM BLAKE (1757–1827)

286 **The Nile flood** In ancient Egypt the central event of the agricultural year was the annual flood of the Nile, which would render the fields fertile. The Egyptians held festivals to celebrate this event, offering food and dedicating poetry to the flood, known as the "illuminator coming out of the darkness". Pay homage to the creative flow that illuminates your darkness. Meditate on the many gifts it brings into your life.

287 **A stream of ideas** "Straightaway the ideas flow in upon me, directly from God." JOHANNES BRAHMS (1833–97)

288 **Draw spontaneously** Give yourself free rein to draw whatever images suggest themselves to you. Try not to censure what comes, simply express whatever surfaces from your consciousness. Now spend some time meditating on the images that you have drawn. In doing so, you may discover a deeper level of self, authentically expressed in the drawing.

If you are feeling adventurous, **paint spontaneously (289)**, or use another artistic medium, such as clay, to express yourself.

290   Your personal helicon In antiquity poets often journeyed to Mount Helicon (a great mountain in central Greece) in search of divine inspiration. They believed that this sacred site was blessed by the nine Muses – the sacred spirits of inspiration. Close your eyes and reflect on your personal helicon – someone among your friends and family who inspires you to express yourself. Bring that person to mind and imagine talking to them. Feel revitalized and inspired by their presence.

291   Soar like a kite Paradoxically, the more connected we are to the earth, the higher our imagination can fly. Imagine that you are a kite, soaring high above the clouds, revelling in glorious surrender to the wind. At the same time become aware of the string that anchors you to the ground, holding you safe.

292   A rainbow bath Visualize yourself standing inside a rainbow, bathing in its explosion of colour. Imagine the different hues, spun out of the spirit's beauty. When you are ready emerge rejuvenated by the life-enhancing light.

PATIENCE

293 Infinite expectations "We must learn to reawaken and keep ourselves awake, not by mechanical aid, but by an infinite expectation of the dawn." HENRY DAVID THOREAU (1817–62)

294 The mulberry leaf "With time and patience the mulberry leaf becomes a silk gown." CHINESE PROVERB

295 A clockless world Sit comfortably and visualize a place where clocks have yet to be invented, where people are free to move according to the natural rhythms of their bodies. Imagine how it would feel to live in this land. Notice the absence of tension, the freedom from expectation, the sense of limitless patience. Try to carry these feelings over into your daily life.

296 The power of patience "Our patience will achieve more than our force." EDMUND BURKE (1729–97)

297 Finding solace "There is nothing so bitter that a patient mind cannot find some solace for it." SENECA (c.4BCE–65CE)

298 **Instant results** Infinite patience creates instant results.

299 **Mixing patience** When we move inward during meditation, we discover every possible quality of spirit. Imagine these qualities as colours on a paint palette. To produce patience first mix peace and love to create faith. Finish by adding a drop of unconditional acceptance. Now imagine yourself using this shade to paint the interior of your psyche.

Mind
and body

THE OBSERVING MIND

300 **Surrender to the mind** "To the mind that is still, the whole universe surrenders." LAO TZU (C.604–531BCE)

301 **Mind and world** Meditate on the paradoxical relationship between mind and world. Your mind is in the world, while at the same time the world is in your mind. See this paradox as the basic mystery and miracle of human life. Hold it in your understanding. What is inside is outside, what is outside is inside. Repeat this sentence over to yourself many times, each time making the two-way mental switch that the words imply.

302 **Hidden wonders** "Recognize what is before your eyes, and what is hidden will be revealed to you." THE GOSPEL OF THOMAS

303 **Maintain your focus** This exercise will help you to develop greater concentration. **1** Choose an everyday object, such as a glass or a pencil, for the focus of your meditation. **2** Sit comfortably, with the object clearly visible in front of you. **3** Close your eyes and spend a few moments becoming aware of your breathing. **4** Now open your eyes and focus softly on the object. Observe your mind's attempts to distract your attention – perhaps with memories, fantasies or anxieties about the future. Whenever you notice yourself drifting in this way, gently return your focus to the object. **5** Continue this exercise for two to three minutes. With practice you will be able to increase the length of this meditation as your mental discipline improves.

304 **Inner mastery** "Be master of mind, rather than mastered by mind." EASTERN SAYING

305 **Breath sensations** This meditation draws your senses inward, helping you to develop concentration. **1** Sit comfortably with your eyes closed. **2** Focus your senses on the physical action of breathing: hear the rushing sounds of the breath; smell the air as it passes through your nostrils; experience the gentle expansion and contraction of your chest cavity; visualize each breath as it flows in and out of your lungs. **3** If you notice that your mind has wandered, gently return your focus to the breath.

306 **The accepting sky** "The almighty sky does not hinder white clouds in their flight." RYOKAN (1758–1831)

307 **Passing clouds** This meditation will help you to cultivate non-attachment. **1** Sit comfortably and close your eyes. **2** Focus your attention on your breathing to ground yourself within your body. **3** As thoughts enter your awareness, observe them without judgment or attachment. Simply allow them to pass across the surface of your mind like clouds across a sky.

308 **In the still depths** "Like weary waves, thought flows upon thought, but the still depth beneath is all thine own." GEORGE MACDONALD (1824–1905)

309 **Going astray** "Wordiness and the intellect; the more we cling to them, the further astray we go." HUI NENG (638–713)

310 **Thought-watching** Rather than identifying with your thoughts, see if you can take a step back and observe them neutrally as they flit across your consciousness. Pretend that you are a bird-watcher – what species of thoughts are flying past? Are they bright and cheerful, or tinged with grey? What patterns of movement do they exhibit? Learn their roosting places, their habits, their strategies of evasion.

311 Moments of clarity "If moment by moment you can keep your mind clear, then nothing will confuse you." SHENG YEN (B.1931)

312 Dream weaving Our dreams can give us insights into situations that we are dealing with in our waking lives. When trying to understand a dream, there is a temptation to rush into an obvious interpretation without allowing time for alternative meanings to suggest themselves. To counteract this tendency, spend time contemplating the dream and the various symbols contained within it. Consider the dream scenario from the perspectives of each of the characters in the dream. Allow a multitude of meanings to emerge from this contemplation.

313 **In the spaces** "Stop
thinking and talking about
it and there is nothing you
will not be able to know."
ZEN PARADOX

314 **Conducting the
orchestra** The Italian
psychoanalyst Roberto
Assagioli likened the
psyche to an orchestra
comprising different
instruments, or
sub-personalities. Once
we become aware of these
different parts of ourselves,
we take on the role of
conductor – able to
orchestrate our separate

parts to produce a tune of our own choosing, rather than being unconsciously controlled by a particular part at any one time. Reflect on your dominant sub-personalities. One way to do this is to observe your thoughts without judgment. Identify the characters behind some of their voices – for example, the plaintive voice of a needy child, the harsh voice of a slave-driver, the loving voice of a nurturing mother. Listen respectfully to each voice in turn – each has something valuable to offer you. Repeated over time this exercise will help you to identify more of your different sub-personalities, raising your self-awareness and giving you more control over your actions.

315 A multitude of reflections "The moon is one, but on agitated water it produces many reflections. Similarly, ultimate reality is one, yet it appears to be many in a mind agitated by thoughts." *MAHARAMAYANA* (11TH CENTURY)

316 Between two chairs Whenever you feel confused or are indecisive, it is often because there is a conflict between two different selves. To resolve such conflicts, imagine a dialogue between the two sides. Visualize two chairs facing each other. Imagine sitting in the first chair and viewing the situation from the perspective of the self with which you feel most closely allied. Explain the position of that self to the other. Then move into the other chair and explain the situation from the perspective of the second self. Continue the dialogue between the two selves, until both have had their say. Now imagine standing back from the two chairs and seeing both selves in relation to each other. What understanding have you gleaned from hearing both sides speak? Can you envision a way to reach reconciliation?

317 The still pool "Give your thoughts a chance to settle down. Then feel your mind clear like a still forest pool." THE BUDDHA (c.563–c.460BCE)

318 Counsel yourself Although we may ask others for advice when we have a problem, usually we already know the answers. This meditation will help you to trust this inner knowing. Sit comfortably, close your eyes and visualize a mirror image of yourself – your alter ego – sitting opposite you. Imagine explaining your problem fully to your alter ego. Elaborate as much as possible, being as honest as you can. When you have finished listen to your alter ego's response. Don't dwell on what your alter ego "should" be saying: simply allow the words to come. Your alter ego is speaking from your higher self and will be able to see through your most self-deceptive strategies.

319 Loosen the chain "Just as a bicycle chain may be too tight, so may one's carefulness and conscientiousness be so tense as to hinder the running of one's mind."
WILLIAM JAMES (1842–1910)

MANAGING EMOTIONS

320 **Stillness and change** In the heart of Australia, a vast mound of rock, called Ayers Rock, rises above the desert plain. As conditions change throughout the day, the rock's hues vary from pinks and golds to reds and indigos – shifts that belie the quiet stillness of the rock itself. As you contemplate this scene, resolve to embody the rock's qualities in your daily activities – still and strong beneath the changing face of your emotions.

321 **Let go of your emotions** Emotions can feel uncontrollable – we have no choice but to experience them. But to live by our emotions is to live under a tyrant's rule. Acknowledge emotions for what they are, without shame or guilt, and then allow them to pass through you like wind moving through the leaves of a tree. Remember that it is only with your permission that feelings can change the way you behave.

322 **Watch the wild horses** We all know what it feels like to have a surge of emotions – and to be aware of how we act on them. See if you can learn to look at emotions from the outside

– in the way that you observe your thoughts while meditating. This experience is like watching wild horses – you sense the strength of their will, but you know that it is safer to stand aside than attempt to mount them.

323   **The flowering of pain**   Difficulties, whether in the form of difficult emotions, people or situations, are like struggling plants. Rather than casting them aside, we must attend to them, trusting in their potential. Water their twisted roots with tears of compassion. Bathe their leaves in the light and warmth of unconditional love. Watch as the plant grows strong and healthy to bear flowers of beauty and fruits of insight.

324   **Reflect on ripples**   This meditation will help you to let go of past pain so that you can move forward with your life. **1** Sitting comfortably, close your eyes and imagine that you are standing by a lake. **2** From the shore choose a stone to represent an event from your past

that causes feelings of discomfort. **3** Imagine throwing the stone into the lake and watching the ripples spreading in concentric circles across the surface. **4** Allow any emotions provoked by your memory of the event to ripple freely through your body, before subsiding without trace. Like the surface of the lake you are now perfectly calm. By experiencing your feelings without resistance, you can let them go and move forward.

325 **Ocean depths** "Like an ocean wave, my emotions come and go, but the depth of my being remains unchanging, eternal." MODERN AFFIRMATION

326 **Holding the child** A common response to emotional pain is to push it away. However, such repression merely causes it to go underground, where it grows stronger, distorting our thoughts in hidden ways. Instead, visualize your emotional pain as a crying child. Imagine holding that child tenderly and lovingly, soothing her with gentle words until the pain dies down.

327 **The headland** The Roman Emperor Marcus Aurelius advises us to "be like the headland against which waves break over and over again. The headland stands strong, until in due course the waters' tumult around it subsides to rest once more." Be strong and patient until your emotions subside.

328 **Cloudy moods** Moods pass through us like clouds across the sky. Allow them to pass, knowing that clear azure blue is the true colour of the spirit. All moods are transient, whether stormy and racing; heavy, dull and slow-moving; or a wispy veil that hides the sun.

329 **The maze of fire** Problems charged with emotion can be particularly difficult to solve because our judgment is often clouded. Imagine navigating through a maze of hedges. When difficult feelings come up, the hedges burst into flames. Keep

this image in mind when you are tackling the problem. Your aim is to find the heart of the maze, to resolve the problem. Difficult emotions may damage your prospect of success. Be analytical and calm. Avoid being singed by the flames.

330 **The broken gong** "If you rest in the stillness like a broken gong, you have already reached heaven, for anger has left you." *DHAMMAPADA*, PART OF THE *PALI CANON* (C.500BCE–0)

331 **Relax with incense** In the brain the processing of smell is closely linked with memory retrieval, so that a smell can act as a powerful trigger for a memory and therefore a mood. This makes it possible to prime calm states of mind using certain scents – helpful when preparing for meditation. Perform this exercise for the first time when you are already feeling calm. Sit comfortably, light some incense and close your eyes. As you breathe focus your awareness on the smell of the incense as it enters your nostrils during each inhalation. Visualize the smell as a beautiful light, flooding your body with liquid calm. Continue

for at least five minutes. Perform this exercise at the start of your meditation practice if you are feeling agitated. Not only will it be calming in itself, but it will also trigger memories of the calm that you experienced the first time around.

332 **The solace of music** "My heart, which is so full to overflowing, has often been solaced and refreshed by music when sick and weary." MARTIN LUTHER (1483–1546)

333 **Musical landscapes** Certain types of music can help to balance your emotions in readiness for meditation. Choose the music according to your mood: an uplifting piece if you are feeling lethargic; a calming piece if you are feeling excitable or agitated. As you listen give your imagination free rein, observing the flow of images that pass through your consciousness in response to the music.

334 **Releasing negativity** Close your eyes and focus your attention on the breath. As you inhale visualize yourself

drawing pure white light in through your nostrils until it fills
your being. As you exhale visualize all your negative thoughts
and painful emotions passing out of your nostrils in a muddy
stream. Maintain this visualization as you continue breathing.

335 **Solve it by walking** There's a famous Latin motto, *Solvitur
ambulando*, which means "Solve it by walking." When faced
with difficult feelings, take a walk for at least twenty minutes –
ideally in a natural setting such as a park, a wood or among
hills. Adjust your mind to the rhythm of your footsteps. Allow
any erroneous thoughts to be jostled out of the basket you are
carrying inside your head and fall by the wayside. By the end
of your walk you will see things in a truer perspective.

336 **Channelling energies** "I am committed to finding the most
worthwhile routes for my energies – I will work to transform my
emotions into the exhilarating
energies of the spirit."
MODERN AFFIRMATION

EMBODIMENT

337 **Kinhin** This Soto Zen meditation, known as *kinhin*, increases awareness of the connections between mind and body. **1** Find a place outside where you can walk for about ten feet (3m) in a straight line. **2** Place your right fist, with thumb inside, just above your navel, and cover it with your left palm. Keep your elbows at right angles. **3** Walk slowly, stepping forward six inches (15cm) each time. Synchronize breath and movement. Inhale as you lift your rear foot, exhale as you push it forward. Focus on your movements and the feel of the ground.

338 **Mindful activity** "When walking, walk. When sitting, sit. But don't wobble!" ZEN PROVERB

339 **Sense your body** Lie on your back with your arms by your sides, eyes closed. Focusing on your toes, tense your muscles for three seconds and then release. Begin to shift your awareness up your body, repeating this action with the main muscle groups of the legs, arms, abdomen, chest, shoulders, neck and head. Now expand your awareness so that your attention encompasses the sensations of your whole body. Enjoy the sense of being fully present in and at one with your body.

340   **Attune to touch** Sit comfortably and close your eyes. Bring your attention to the surface on which you are sitting. Notice how it supports your sitting bones. Expand your awareness to encompass the touch of your clothes on your skin. How do they feel? Can you differentiate between fabrics? Sensitizing yourself to touch will help you to feel more present in your body.

341   **Meditative massage** Performing this visualization prior to meditation will help to release tension, making it easier to sit still during your practice. Sit comfortably and close your eyes. Imagine that someone is massaging your shoulders. Feel the knots release and your shoulders drop. Now imagine your masseur releasing the tension in other parts of your body. Continue the visualization until you feel relaxed and at ease.

As an alternative, imagine **massaging a loved one (342)**. Visualize love flowing down your arms into the other person.

343 **Live in the world** "Seclude the mind, not the movements, remain living in the world of man and woman. Lack a tree? Plant a sapling. Without a mountain? Look at a picture. Living amid noise, I am not flustered. True meaning is found in this." CHIAO-JAN (730–799)

344 **Spiritual sight** The sensory experience of seeing relates to the spiritual quality of insight. To access this quality bring your awareness to what you can see, for example, by concentrating on an object in front of you. Then close your eyes and draw your attention inward. Holding your eyes in your awareness, use them imaginatively to sense inward rather than outward. What can you see with your inner eye? With practice this technique will help you to develop greater insight.

Apply this technique to your **hearing (345)** to access calm thoughts, and to **feeling (346)** to access your intuition.

347 **Awareness in the moment** "When breathing in a long breath, [the meditator] knows that he breathes in a long breath;

when breathing in a short breath, he knows that he breathes in a short breath." *ANAPANASATI SUTRA* (C.300–C.100BCE)

348 **Stars and sunshine** "The human body is vapour, materialized by sunshine and mixed with the life of the stars." PARACELSUS (1493–1541)

349 **The complete breath** This is a form of yogic meditation in which deep breathing is synchronized with arm movements to unite mind and body. **1** Lie on your back with arms out to the sides. **2** Close your eyes and focus on breathing through your nose. **3** Inhale for five counts and exhale for ten. **4** Repeat three times, noticing the sense of relaxation that permeates your body. **5** Take five more breaths, this time raising your arms over your head as you inhale and returning your arms to your sides as you exhale.

350 **Balance** "When you stand with your two feet on the ground, you will always keep your balance." LAO TZU (C.604–531BCE)

351 **Breath and mind** "When the breath is irregular, the mind is also unsteady; but when the breath is still, so is the mind." *HATHAYOGAPRADIPIKA* (14TH CENTURY)

352 **Heart rhythms** Meditating on our heartbeat brings us into contact with the pulse of life expressed in our bodies. Sit comfortably in a quiet environment. Close your eyes and place your hand on the left side of your chest. As you become aware of your heart's beating, you may also just begin to hear its sound as the blood pulses through your ears. At the same time try to visualize the heart as it pumps the blood all around your body. Hold that image in your mind, allowing your consciousness to fuse with the pulsing energy of the life-force as it passes through you.

353 **The creative dancer** "Imagine then a dancer who, after long study, prayer and inspiration, has attained such a degree of understanding that his body is simply the luminous manifestation of his soul; whose body dances in accordance with

a music heard inwardly, in an expression of something out
of another, profounder world. This is the truly creative dancer
... speaking in movement out of himself and out of something
greater than all selves." ISADORA DUNCAN (1878–1927)

354   **Soul dance** Meditative moving from within – from impulses
that arise from the unconscious rather than the conscious mind –
is a form of what Jung called "active imagination". This is a
process whereby unconscious material is brought into conscious
awareness through the creative act. Find a clear space and curl
up in the fetal position on the floor. Close your eyes and bring
your awareness to the sensations within your body. When
you feel ready, allow yourself to move, following the inner
promptings of your body rather than directing the movement
with your ego. Observe any feelings that arise as you move.

355   **On both sides of the mirror** "The Self exists both inside
and outside the physical body, just as an image exists inside
and outside the mirror." *ASHTAVAKRA GITA* (c.200BCE–c.200CE)

— SUBTLE ENERGIES —

356   **The subtle body** We all have two bodies – our physical body and our subtle body. Our subtle body is a body of light, which envelops our form. Sitting quietly, close your eyes and visualize your subtle body. Imagine standing up in your subtle body and walking a short distance, leaving your physical self behind. Turn to look at your physical self sitting in the chair. Notice how detached yet aware you feel, and how peaceful your mind.

Next time take **a longer walk (357)** in your subtle body, or imagine **flying (358)**, as your subtle body is weightless.

359   **Vowel tones** Mystic traditions teach that each vowel corresponds to an energy point within the body. Each centre is opened and energized by sounding the vowel that is its "seed sound" in a process called toning. To begin toning sing the vowels "A, E, I, O, U" starting at middle C and going up to G. Then repeat the sequence of notes with your mouth closed. This creates internal vibrations, which help to release energy blocks and balance the *chakras*.

When you become more practised, try these variations: with your mouth closed, vary the position of your tongue to project the sound up into your nasal cavity, creating a **buzzing sound (360)**; form your lips into a rounded kiss and project the sound through them to make a sound resembling **whale calls (361)**.

362 **Alternate nostril breathing** This exercise manipulates the flow of energy through the *nadis* (energy channels) in the body. **1** To alter the flow of air through your nostrils, use the thumb of your right hand to close your right nostril and inhale through your left nostril. **2** Release the thumb, and use the ring and little finger of your right hand to close your left nostril while exhaling through your right nostril. **3** Now inhale through your right nostril. Then close your right nostril with your thumb, release your ring and little fingers and exhale through your left nostril. **4** Repeat this cycle eight times.

363 **The throat chakra** Visualize a blue spinning disk at the front of your throat. This will unblock the *vishuddha* throat *chakra*,

which is associated with shades of blue. This is helpful if you find it difficult to express yourself verbally.

Taking this exercise a stage further, lie on your back and place a small **blue stone or crystal (364)** at the base of your throat. Closing your eyes, focus on the stone. Imagine its power activating the vortex of energy at your throat.

365 Rainbow meditation

Colours are waves of light energy that have direct physiological and psychological effects. We can use them in meditation to influence our feelings and perceptions. To perform this meditation, choose a hue that represents the qualities you would like to cultivate in that particular moment (see p.192). Then cut a square or circle from a piece of paper or fabric in that shade and use the shape as a focus for your meditation.

Alternatively, focus on a **coloured object (366)**, allowing the colour rather than the form to dominate your consciousness, or **visualize a colour (367)**, allowing it to fill your mind.

368 **Crystal meditation** Possessing subtle energies that influence our feelings and perceptions, crystals provide an ideal focus for meditation. Follow your intuition when choosing your crystal – the stone with the qualities you need will draw your attention.

Alternatively, match your situation with the profile of a crystal. Purple **amethyst (369)** possesses healing properties. Green **aventurine (370)** calms chaotic thoughts. **Carnelian (371)**, which ranges in hue from orange to red, increases energy and motivation. **Clear quartz (372)** offers strength and protection. **Rose quartz (373)** encourages self-acceptance and the belief that we are worthy of love. **Sodalite (374)** – a blue stone, flecked with white – brings mental clarity and aids expression. **Tiger's eye (375)** – a brown stone marked with bands of yellow – inspires courage and confidence. **Yellow calcite (376)** lifts depression, bringing inner strength and peace.

HEALING THE PSYCHE

377   **Friendship** According to the Bible, "A faithful friend is the medicine of life." A good friend will always ease your burdens. Fill your life with such friends, offering them your love and support in return. Think of them often: their healing powers are priceless.

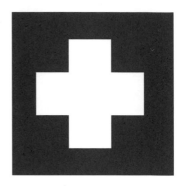

378   **Heal your wounds** The deepest wounds in our psyche are inflicted by ourselves. It is not a person's insult that hurts us so much as the act of replaying the insult, which deepens the wound. To heal psychic scars we must apply the ointment of understanding and compassion, and the healing compress of love. In a meditative state of mind, first reflect on a painful psychic wound. Recognize how you have deepened it through

mental repetition. Resolve to forgive yourself and send
the vibration of forgiveness to the wounder. Now focus on
irradiating your wound with light. Feel the pain dissipate.

379 **Silent retreat** "True silence is the rest of the mind; it is to
the spirit what sleep is to the body, nourishment and
refreshment." WILLIAM PENN (1644–1718)

380 **Out of captivity** Emotions are essentially
energy in motion. When emotions are repressed,
energy is blocked, with damaging repercussions
for the health of mind and body.
Visualize wild animals trapped
in a cage. What emotions do
they represent and why are
you so afraid of them? Do their
postures in the cage resemble
your own behaviour in any way?
Now imagine releasing the animals.

Watch them run off into the distance, finally disappearing
as tiny specks on the horizon. Now you are free.

381 Healing arrows Emotional wounds are the instruments
by which we heal others. Meditate on your deepest wound.
Imagine the arrow there, embedded in your flesh. Painfully pull
out the arrow and use it as a wand to touch someone beside
you. As your arrow touches them, their own wound begins to
heal. Experience your suffering as a source of healing energies.

382 Baptism of suffering "Deep unspeakable suffering may
well be called a baptism, a regeneration, the initiation into
a new state." GEORGE ELIOT (1819–80)

383 Release shame Shame is an emotional response to
humiliation. It becomes toxic when internalized as part of our
identity, causing us to hide our real self from others. To release
toxic shame, take a few deep breaths and turn your attention
inward. Scan your body for nauseating feelings of shame or

self-disgust. Visualize these feelings as a murky green toxin that is polluting your body. Now imagine white light pouring into the crown of your head and flooding through your being. Watch the green dissolve as your body is purified from the inside out. Experience the feelings of nausea subside.

384   **The power of prayer**   "The prayer of the heart is the source of all good, refreshing the soul as if it were a garden." ST GREGORY OF SINAI (D.1360)

385   **The child within**   Many of the emotional wounds that we carry around were inflicted when we were children. One way to heal such wounds is to comfort the child within. Imagine a child standing before you. Gazing down at the child, you realize that it's you when you were small. Kneel down beside the child and introduce yourself. Encourage them to come toward you. If they are willing, hold them close to your heart in a warm embrace. Reassure the child that they are safe in your arms and that you will always be there to protect them from harm.

386   Self-forgiveness When we perform an action that contravenes our moral code, we experience feelings of guilt, which pervade the psyche like the smell of dirty laundry. Washing our psychic laundry is essential for peace of mind. Imagine entering the

house of your psyche. Search each room for dirty laundry and acknowledge the wrongs this laundry represents. Now take the laundry to a tub and wash the fabrics clean in the waters of self-forgiveness. As the dirt washes away, feel your guilt dissipate.

387 **The Divine Child** The Jungian archetype of the Divine Child represents our innate innocence and vulnerability. There is often a temptation to reject these childlike qualities in the quest for maturity. However, if we can cherish these qualities within ourselves, they provide a valuable catalyst for transformation.

388 **A child's heart** "A great man is he who does not lose his child's heart." Meng Tzu (c.372–c.289bce)

389 **Re-parent yourself** Visualize the perfect parents. What qualities would they display? Take time to refine and build your vision each day for a week. When your vision is complete, introduce yourself to your imaginary parents and begin to cultivate a loving relationship.

COPING WITH ILLNESS

390 **Talking with pain** When we experience physical pain, the body is sending us a message. Yet, all too often we suppress the pain without learning anything from it. Next time you feel pain in your body, take a moment to visualize it in physical form. Ask your pain what it is trying to tell you. It may be warning you of an underlying physical problem, or perhaps indicating a hidden emotional issue. Heed its advice.

391 **Limbo** Awaiting the results of a health test can be a very stressful period in which we feel like we are in limbo. At such times it is important to remember that life is not suspended, but continues as before. Although the body may be flagging, the spirit remains undimmed. We must accept that we cannot expect perfection, only to continue, for the spirit leases a beautiful house in the earthquake zone.

392 **Mind relief** "Rather than give the body relief, give relief to the mind: when the mind is at peace, the body is not distressed." MUMON (1900–1988)

393 **The animal inside** On one level
curing illness depends upon
healing the soul. As the soul
thrives on imagination, a
good way to heal sickness is
to apply imagination to your
symptoms. Bring your
awareness into the present
moment and try to visualize your
illness as an animal. Observe the
animal's actions. If you feel
compelled to interact with
it, feel free to do so. What
clues do the species and
mood of the animal
give you about the
nature of your illness and
how you may be able
to heal yourself?

394 Healing thoughts We can help the healing process in meditation by creating positive thoughts that support the immune system. Quietly surrender yourself to the process of healing. Send your body the gift of loving thoughts. Imagine those thoughts penetrating your cells giving them the strength they need to heal. Envision your body returned to health.

395 The eye of Horus Horus was the Egyptian god of the sky. He was depicted as a falcon, his left eye represented by the moon, his right eye by the sun. According to myth the light of the moon eye restored the dismembered body of the god Osiris (who had been murdered by his brother) to life in the underworld. Meditate on the eye of Horus, bringing wholeness into your life.

396 Hands-on healing We can use our hands to channel healing energies into areas of the body where there is pain or disease – for ourselves as well as for other people. First, bring your awareness into your hands to bring a warmth and sensitivity to your touch. Place your hands upon the affected part of your

body. Close your eyes and visualize white healing energy
passing in through the top of your head, down your arms and
hands, and then into the body. You may feel tingling in your
hands. Continue for five minutes, or until the pain eases.

397 Soul profits "There is nothing the body suffers which the soul
may not profit by." GEORGE MEREDITH (1828–1909)

398 Healing temple Visualize a place that you find healing –
perhaps your childhood bedroom or a beloved holiday resort.
Visit this place in your mind to comfort you when you are sick.

399 The balancing mudra Perform the *matangi mudra* (see p.86)
at the beginning of your meditation practice to restore balance
to your mind and body. Clasp your hands together and place
them at the level of your solar plexus. Release your two middle
fingers, extend them and bring them together to form a point.
With your eyes closed hold this *mudra* for a few minutes,
observing any thoughts and feelings that arise.

WELL-BEING

400   **Universal flow** "The energy of the universe flows through me, maintaining my well-being. I release energy in ways that are healing for myself and the Earth." MODERN AFFIRMATION

401   **Life's wonders** "Everything is extraordinarily clear. I see the whole landscape before me. I see my hands, my feet, my toes, and I smell the rich river mud. I feel a great sense of strangeness and wonder at being alive." THE BUDDHA (c.563–c.460BCE)

402   **Find wholeness** To find "wholeness" is to be aware of all that we are and all that is available to us. This involves celebrating mind, body and spirit. To do justice to the mind, use reason as a tool, constructively and creatively. To do justice to the body, foster well-being and be aware of your kinship with all living things. To do justice to the spirit, be loving, revere the infinite mystery that gives life its meaning and live by the spirit's values.

403   **Wholeness** "Be really whole and all things will come to you." LAO-TZU (c.604–531BCE)

404   **Fire breathing** This practice raises *prana* (the life-force), and is said to oxygenate the blood, cleanse the organs and tone the system. Perform this technique prior to your daily meditation so that your body receives a work-out as well as your mind. Take a deep breath, filling your lungs. Exhale in quick snorts, rapidly contracting and releasing your stomach muscles. Continue for a minute or two, stopping if you experience discomfort.

405   **Stillness** "You must learn to be still in the midst of activity and to be vibrantly alive in repose." MAHATMA GANDHI (1869–1948)

406   **The gift of energy** Giving positive energy to others while expecting nothing in return invokes spiritual well-being. During your morning meditation, prepare for the day's giving by imagining the energy of the cosmos flowing into all of your being. Afterwards, reflect on the day ahead. In each interaction imagine giving your energy, attention and appreciation without wishing for anything in return. Plan to take breaks throughout the day in which to recharge your spiritual batteries.

407   **The archetypes** According to Jung, gender identity is influenced by archetypes: for a man – Warrior, Lover, Magician and King; for a woman – Amazon, Heteira (love goddess), Wise Woman and Mother. The psyche of an individual contains all four archetypes, but often he or she will identify primarily with one of them, rejecting the others. For Jung, the journey to psychic wholeness involves befriending *all* the archetypes, recognizing the role that each one plays in our lives. Close your eyes and imagine that all four are standing before you. Introduce yourself to each. Begin with the one you feel most comfortable with and progress to the more difficult. Repeat this exercise on a regular basis. As you become more acquainted with each archetype, you will gradually be able to embrace their influence in your life.

408   **Release tension** Lying comfortably, close your eyes. Scan through your body to locate any areas of tension. Breathe into each of these areas, visualizing your breath as white light that surrounds and dissolves the tension. Continue until your body is flooded with white light and filled with relaxation.

409 **Sun breath** Practise this deep-breathing technique before meditation to relieve physical tension. Stand with your hands by your sides. Breathe into your belly while stretching out your arms. Then breathe into your mid-chest and bring your hands into a prayer position at your heart. Lift your hands over your head and breathe into your upper chest. As you exhale lower your hands to your sides. Repeat nine times.

410 **Three-stage breathing** This breathing exercise slows and deepens the breath, aiding breath control and inducing a meditative state. **1** Sitting comfortably, close your eyes and place one palm on your belly and one on your chest. **2** Inhale air into your belly for three counts, then into your chest for three counts, and then into your throat for three counts. **3** Then exhale from your belly for three counts, from your chest for three counts, and from your throat for three counts. Notice the movements of your hands to ensure that you are breathing correctly. **4** Repeat this exercise nine times.

411 **The sacred garment** "The body is a sacred garment. It's your first and last garment; it is what you enter life in and what you depart life with, and it should be treated with honor." MARTHA GRAHAM (1894–1991)

412 **Essential oils** The essential oils of plants can have powerful effects on our emotional states. They can be used alone or in blends for inhalation, massage, compresses, baths and in special burners. However you decide to use an essential oil, spend some time focusing on the scent to receive its full benefits.

Certain essential oils are particularly good for inducing relaxation and are helpful when preparing for meditation: apple-scented **chamomile (413)** has a soothing effect on the nerves and is suitable for sensitive skins; woody-smelling **frankincense (414)** has a calming effect and aids relaxation; **jasmine (415)** has a sweet scent, and acts as an antidepressant; fresh-scented **lavender (416)** has analgesic and calming properties and treats insomnia, depression, aches, pains and wounds; sweet-smelling **neroli (417)** is comforting and can be used to treat anxiety and insomnia; exotic **ylang ylang (418)** has antidepressant and sedative properties, and allays anxiety.

419 **Daily renewal** "Renew yourself completely each day; do it again, and again, and again, forever again." CHINESE SAYING

420 **Relax with music** According to scientific research, music with a slow beat, such as a Gregorian chant, induces relaxation by regulating brainwave patterns. When listening to such music, close your eyes and allow the sounds to fill your body, washing away any tension or feelings of unease.

421 **The sleep mudra** Practising the *shakti mudra* (see p.86) before bedtime will help you to wind down and relax. Sitting comfortably, tuck your thumbs into your palms, curl your index and middle fingers around them and bring your hands together so that the tops of your little and ring fingers touch. Close your eyes, bring your attention inward and allow your breathing and thoughts to slow down. Hold this *mudra* for five to ten minutes.

422 **The path of peace** "Harmony is eating and resting, sleeping and waking: balance in all you do. This is the path to peace."
BHAGAVAD GITA (1ST OR 2ND CENTURY)

423 **Prime your sleep with images** Some people are able to cue restful dreams by meditating on an image that they associate with happiness or peace – perhaps an image of home, a soothing landscape or a cherished friend – for a few minutes before bed. As they meditate on the image, it penetrates the unconscious where it can help to ward off troubled dreams.

Home
and family

424 **The decision** "Making the decision to have a child – it's momentous. It is to decide forever to have your heart go walking outside your body." ELIZABETH STONE (20TH CENTURY)

425 **Womb's wisdom** This meditation is for a pregnant mother. Sit comfortably and place your hands over your womb. Visualize the course of your pregnancy as the inexorable current of a river flowing from spring to delta. Imagine the burbling waters as your infant's first sounds. See the river enriched with minerals from the land over which it flows – the nutrients of your own life-giving body. Have faith in the natural process of pregnancy.

At seven months the unborn child is almost fully formed in the womb, with eyelashes, fingerprints and well-developed hearing. At this point many cultures around the world hold ceremonies to celebrate the new life unfolding and prepare the child for entry into the world. To conduct your own ceremony, close your eyes and visualize and describe aloud the details of **your home (426)** – both as a calming meditation for yourself and as a symbolic treat for the unborn baby.

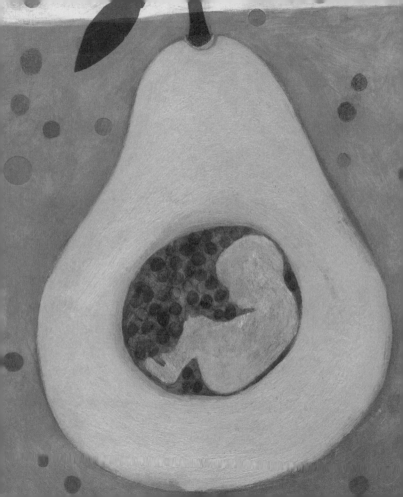

427 **To an unborn child** This meditation is for either parent of an unborn child. Close your eyes and visualize the child lying curled up in the womb. Imagine soft, loving energy flowing from your heart into the womb and surrounding the child in a warm embrace. Make a silent promise to your child that you will care for them and protect them to the best of your ability.

428 **A miracle** "Before you were conceived I wanted you. Before you were born I loved you. Before you were here an hour I would die for you. This is the miracle of life." MAUREEN HAWKINS (20TH CENTURY)

429 **Modron** In the Celtic tradition the figure of the archetypal Mother is called Modron. Women can draw on the support of Modron to assist them with mothering. Imagine yourself in a sunlit glade. Before you sits Modron, crowned with wild roses. Her calm eyes smile at you, inviting you to sit beside her. She promises that she will protect and nurture you, so that you can offer love to others. Her sweet breath enfolds you in a scented cloud. You close your eyes and absorb her love. When you open them you are back in the everyday world, resolved to offer her love to others.

430 **A midwife's blessing** "A little drop of the sky, a little drop of the land, a little drop of the sea, on your forehead, beloved one. To protect, to shield and to surround you. The little drop of the Three, to fill you with the graces." TRADITIONAL CELTIC PRAYER

431 **The miracle of new life** "In awe I watch you, your tiny chest rising and falling in the depths of sleep. I am overwhelmed by the love I feel for you. That I should have assisted in your creation seems inconceivable to me. As I look at you, the miracle that is life becomes clear. My gratitude is profound." MODERN AFFIRMATION

432 **A child again** "You should study not only that you become a mother when your child is born, but also that you become a child." DOGEN (1200–1253)

433 **Your journey together** Cradling your baby in your arms, gaze lovingly upon their small form and consider the ways in which you are at once alike and yet different from one another. Contemplate your future journey together – a voyage of discovering your selves, each other, and the world.

434 **A fresh bud** "I lift up this newborn child to you. You brought it to birth, you gave it life. This child is a fresh bud on an ancient tree, a new member of an old family. May this fresh bud blossom. May this child grow strong and righteous." KALAHARI BUSHMEN'S SONG, AFRICA

435 **The rock in the river** While your child is five years of age or under, take time each day to play the game of "the rock in the river". To do this sit cross-legged on the floor and invite your child to sit on your legs with their back to your chest. Enfold them gently in your arms and encourage them to be still with you for five minutes. With time they will develop a sense of inner stillness that will stay with them for the rest of their life.

436 Roots and wings "There are only two lasting bequests we can hope to give our children. One is roots; the other, wings." HODDING CARTER (1907–1972)

437 Demeter's legacy Greek mythology describes the abduction of Persephone by Hades, Lord of the Underworld, and the experiences of her mother Demeter, as she seeks to retrieve her daughter from captivity. This story explores the dilemma faced by many parents as their children go out into the world. Although they wish to protect their children from danger, an important task of parenting involves allowing children to explore their own depths and the mystery of fate – which draws them into the potentially dangerous but transformative experiences of life.

LEARNING AND GROWTH

438 **Acorn potential** Meditate on the potential of an acorn. Visualize it growing into a great oak tree over the course of many decades. Imagine how the world around the tree will change during that time. Now focus on the potential within yourself. Imagine yourself growing into that potential self during the course of your life, surrounded by a changing world.

439 **Cracking** "As I begin to explore new territories of the self, the shell of my false self-image begins to fracture under the pressure of my growth. I emerge – a newly hatched chick. I look forward to the adventure of learning." MODERN AFFIRMATION

440 **In the womb** This meditation takes you back to the womb where your growth first began. Close your eyes and imagine yourself lying curled up as a fetus. Your body feels weightless, supported by warm fluid. You feel safe and warm, soothed by the soft throb of your mother's heart. You feel yourself growing

and developing, nurtured into a life of joy and potential by
the strength of your mother's love.

441   **A course in miracles** "After you were born, every minute
brought a new miracle: the flowering of a new life, the training
of a new adventurer. May your adventures seem
miraculous to yourself. May you one day know it
is not to me you must give thanks." MODERN
PRAYER FROM SCOTLAND

442   **The best** "The best preacher is the heart;
the best teacher is time; the best book is the
world; the best friend is God." HEBREW PROVERB

443   **Your warrior name** In the shamanic tradition the father
of the tribe is responsible for initiating the young warriors.
Imagine yourself sitting alone at the place of initiation, awaiting
the arrival of the Father. When the Father appears, you rise
in respect. Looking into your eyes, he asks you for your name.

In response, the Father embraces you and whispers your new, warrior name into your ear. A current of energy surges through you – you have crossed from childhood into adulthood, becoming a warrior in your own right. Keep your new name secret; use it as a source of strength when times are difficult.

444 **Seeds of promise** Children are full of promise, and we naturally wish to nurture and support them in their efforts to reach their full potential. However, we can develop at any age. Find the promise within yourself and apply the same kind of care to your own development as you would to that of a child – it's never too late for further growth.

445 **Another time** There is a rabbinical saying: "Don't limit a child to your own learning, for he was born in another time." Give your child the freedom to explore the world for themselves. If you fear for their safety in territories unknown to you, walk beside them and explore those places together. Let your children be your guides in rediscovering the world.

446 **The age for philosophy** "Anyone who claims to be not yet ready or else past the age for philosophy is like the person who claims to be too young or too old for happiness." EPICURUS (C.341–270BCE)

447 **Life-long learning** The aim of life is learning – how to be yourself, how to be good, how to love.

448 **Following great footsteps** List ten great leaders from the last twenty years. Identify the particular gift or quality possessed by each one that inspired others to follow them – for example, Mother Teresa's compassion for others. Each day make one of these gifts or qualities the focus for your meditation. Doing so will encourage them to grow within your character.

449 **Growing pains** The psychologist Carl Jung said that we cannot grow in consciousness without pain. Consider the pain in your life as a growing pain. However old you are you are still growing in wisdom and experience, and the pain of that growing, although it fluctuates in intensity, will always be with you, like your legs that take you every step of your journey.

450 **Cities and circles** "To draw a city, with its ramparts, roofs and chimneys, is easy: a child could do it. To draw a perfect circle takes years of practice." ANDREW PARKER (20TH CENTURY)

451 **Playing the violin** "Life is like playing a violin in public and learning the instrument as one goes on." SAMUEL BUTLER (1835–1902)

452 **The living library** Meditate on a vast library. It is a monument to the greatest minds that have ever existed – for books are living things, which immortalize the most profound thinking of humanity. Even this little book earns its place there, because the library welcomes all books that are well-intentioned. Imagine your own best thoughts living on in the memories of the friends and family to whom you have expressed them. Your words have seeded, rooted and flowered in happy recollections.

453 **Understanding** "Much learning does not teach understanding." HERACLITUS (C.540–C.480BCE)

454 **Wisdom of the family** The family has much to teach us about ourselves and the world. In your mind's eye, visualize a tall tree whose branches reach up into the clouds. Looking up at the tree you see the members of your family sitting on the branches. You begin to climb the tree, stopping to converse with your relatives along the way. Ask them what lessons they have to teach you.

455 **Sharing your light** "If you have knowledge, let others light their candles at it." MARGARET FULLER (1810–50)

THE NURTURING CORE

456 **The support of Anu** In Celtic shamanism Anu is one
of the names given to the archetypal Mother – the goddess
who gave birth to the world and watches over and cares for
all living things. Close your eyes and imagine Anu standing
before you. She is beautiful and graceful, her eyes full of
loving kindness and understanding. She takes you in her
arms and holds you, giving you infinite love and support.

457 **Sacred circle** For each one of us there are certain precious
things – places, people and practices – that support us in being
true to ourselves. For example, a park that you enjoy visiting, a
dear friend who allows you to see yourself reflected in the warm
mirror of their love, a dance class that allows you to express
your creativity and joy for life, a daily meditation practice that
gives you time to be with yourself. Spend a few moments
considering these sources of joy, strength and energy in your
life. It is vitally important to protect these priorities. Visualize
them within a sacred circle and promise yourself that you will
do your best to protect that circle from outside threats.

458 **Finding home** There are certain places in the world where we feel particularly at home – comfortable, nurtured, at ease with ourselves and our surroundings. Close your eyes and bring to mind a place that evokes these feelings in you. As well as visualizing all the details of

the setting, conjure up the sounds and smells, perhaps even the taste of the air. Allow the unique qualities of the place to nourish and relax you. Feel yourself move into harmony with yourself and your environment.

459 **Loaves and lilies** "When you have only two pennies left in the world, buy a loaf of bread with one, and a lily with the other." CHINESE PROVERB

460   Inner resources "I have everything I need for a full, rich, happy life. My inner resources are abundant. I have plenty of support, for which I offer thanks." MODERN AFFIRMATION

461   A waking meditation On waking, perform this meditation while still lying in bed. Eyes closed, imagine that you are lying on the ground where your apartment block or house used to be; the building has vaporized in the night. Visualize the scene around you: houses, backyards, gardens, streets, fields, or whatever. Imagine the sounds and smells you would experience, and the nature of the weather. Complete your meditation by rebuilding your home as an act of imagination. This is what might have been: be thankful for what is.

462   The heart of the home In many cultures, the kitchen is seen as the symbolic heart of the home – a focal point where the family gathers around the fire to prepare, cook and eat food.

One way to purify the heart is to clean the kitchen mindfully. As you scrub the floor, wipe the work-surfaces and wash the tiles, imagine that you are purging any impurities from your heart until it is overflowing with unconditional love.

463 A flower garden "If family minds love one another, the home will be a beautiful flower garden." THE BUDDHA (c.563–c.460BCE)

464 A loaf of bread Close your eyes and visualize a loaf of bread in the oven. In the heat the pale dough slowly expands and browns – a symbol of the home's nurturing warmth. Imagine removing the loaf from the oven and allowing it to cool on a wire rack for a few minutes before cutting yourself a slice. As you eat the warm, fragrant bread, you feel comforted from within: the bread replenishes body and soul.

465 Eat meditatively Instead of eating on the run, give yourself time to relax and enjoy your food. Relish the taste of each

mouthful. As you do so offer gratitude for the food that you are eating – it is a gift from the earth. Respect all those involved in bringing the food to the table – from the farmer through to the cook. Give thanks for the presence of those who share the food with you. By engaging fully in the act of eating, the meal becomes a sacred ritual by which we renew ourselves.

466 **Cooking with love** When prepared with care and attention, food can provide emotional as well as physical sustenance to those who eat it. Before you begin cooking, ritually wash and bless your hands, and clear your mind with three deep breaths. As your prepare the meal, keep in mind the image of those you are feeding, and visualize love passing outward from your heart, along your arms and into the food. Serve it with due ceremony.

467 **Absorbing vital energy** After eating it is good to practise a short meditation to aid the digestive process. Visualize the journey of your meal as it passes through your digestive system. Imagine the enzymes hard at work as they break down the food.

Then imagine the nutrients being absorbed into your blood and transported to every cell in your body. Imagine the cells sparkling with life as they transform the nutrients into energy.

468   **The peace table** Practise this meditation before a family gathering to bring a spirit of goodwill to the occasion. Visualize the dining table with your family members seated around it. Mentally go around the table, stopping at each person in turn to reflect on your relationship with them. Is there any tension between you? How can it be resolved? Imagine yourself settling the differences between you wherever possible. Bring the sense of peace generated by these reconciliations with you to the meal.

469   **A well for others** Throughout our lives people come to us with various needs and desires. In order to meet these needs without becoming exhausted, imagine yourself as a deep well of pure energy. See those around you – family, friends and colleagues – drawing strengths, such as love, peace and wisdom, from your well. Then imagine them leaving you refreshed.

470 **A perfect chord** "The diversity in the family should be the cause of love and harmony, as it is in music where many different notes blend together in the making of a perfect chord." FROM THE BAHA'I SCRIPTURES (19TH CENTURY)

471 **Living in harmony** When we embark on a new experience, we may shiver with fear or sweat with desire. Better to live in harmony, at the temperature of our surroundings.

472 **An imaginary pet** Pets provide us with comfort and companionship. Their presence in our lives has been shown to improve mental well-being. Close your eyes and visualize a pet – either an actual or an imaginary one. Imagine stroking the pet, and as you do so, synchronize your breathing with the rhythm of your stroking, allowing the action to soothe you. Become aware of the bond of companionship between you and the pet.

SACRED SPACES

473 **A warm welcome** "I welcome others into my house. Here is the room I am most proud of – the kitchen, crossroads of friendship and the world's blessings." MODERN AFFIRMATION

474 **Space-clearing** Clearing your home of clutter not only creates more living space but also helps you to let go of mental clutter. Your memories and identifications may be distracting you from the essence of who you are in the present moment. Keep this in mind as you clear out your home, consciously releasing yourself from attachments.

475 **Harmony in the home** "If there is harmony is the house, there will be order in the nation. If there is order in the nation, there will be peace in the world." CHINESE PROVERB

476 **Create a sacred space** A sacred space is a place imbued with uplifting spiritual energy. This may be because many have meditated there or good deeds have been done. We can create a sacred space in the home through our meditation practice.

Find a quiet space with a chair, cushion or mat, and sit down. Close your eyes and fill the space with vibrations of love for your family, of compassion for all who you know are suffering, and of peace for the world. Finally, call upon the One, the source of ultimate truth, to join you in conjuring and sustaining your sacred space.

477 The lord's estate "Happy is the estate that is seen by the eye of its lord." LEONARDO DA VINCI (1452–1519)

478 A reflection of your soul One way to gain a deeper sense of yourself is to meditate on the character of your living environment, which provides a reflection of your soul. Close your eyes and visualize the exterior of your home. Look at it as if you were a stranger, seeing it for the very first time. Hold each detail in mind, allowing the deeper significances to emerge. What is your overriding impression? Repeat this process

for each room inside. Try to move beyond the surfaces to a deeper sense of the spirit of the home.

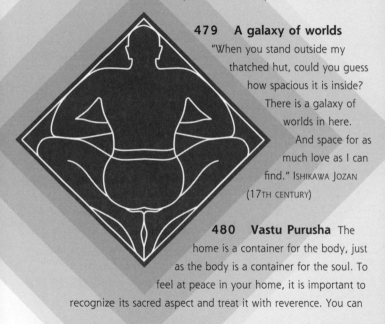

479   A galaxy of worlds

"When you stand outside my thatched hut, could you guess how spacious it is inside? There is a galaxy of worlds in here.
And space for as much love as I can find." ISHIKAWA JOZAN (17TH CENTURY)

480   Vastu Purusha The

home is a container for the body, just as the body is a container for the soul. To feel at peace in your home, it is important to recognize its sacred aspect and treat it with reverence. You can do this by making a tribute to Vastu Purusha – the Vedic spirit of earthly creation and architecture, believed to occupy every home, with his head in the northeast and his folded legs in the southwest. Simply arrange some beautiful fresh flowers in the northeast of your home, reflecting humbly on the spirit of Vastu Purusha as you do so.

481 **An empty vessel** Try this meditation to heighten awareness of your physical space. Visualize the form of an empty teacup and the space into which the tea is poured. Would the cup be a cup without its outer form and inner space? Could the cup exist without the emptiness around it? Reflect on the subtle interplay between form and emptiness in everything around you.

482 **Form and function** "The usefulness of a pot comes from its emptiness." LAO TZU (C.604–531BCE)

483 **Focus on white** White is made up of all the shades of the spectrum and provides the most balanced source of energy.

Meditating on white has a calming and uplifting effect that connects us to the spirit. If you have white walls in your home, sit in front of a blank section and focus on the space in front of you. Allow the reflected white light to fill your consciousness.

Alternatively, you can meditate on walls of different hues to produce different effects on your psyche. **Green (484)** reminds us of nature in full bloom and has a nurturing and harmonizing effect; **yellow (485)** is associated with the sun and promotes optimism, personal power and self-confidence; **orange (486)** stimulates warmth and vitality, boosting motivation and focus; **red (487)** is associated with strength and passion and has a grounding effect; **pink (488)** represents tenderness and compassion and has a soothing effect; **blue (489)** is associated with the sky and promotes clarity, openness and self-expression; **purple (490)** connects us to the source of spiritual power and has a strong healing effect.

491 **Appreciate everything** This meditation gives us the opportunity to appreciate the beauty of even the most commonplace objects – beauty that we often fail to notice amid the barrage of visual impressions to which we are subject. Sit comfortably and take a few breaths to relax your body. Pick up an object – perhaps a book or glass – and place it in front of you. Look at the form carefully, noticing the unique intricacies of shape and the subtle gradations of shading and texture. Practise this process of contemplation with different items. In doing so you will deepen your awareness of the intrinsic value in all things.

492   Mind and matter "Things are objects where there is a subject or mind; and the mind is a subject where there are objects." SOSAN ZENJI (D.606)

493   Create a meditation space Find a place within your home where you can escape from the distractions of the television, the phone and the demands of other people. Embellish this sacred space with some fresh flowers and any natural objects that you find soothing – perhaps stones or rock crystals. Add some soft cushions so that you can sit here and meditate in comfort. Each day spend five minutes in this space simply being with yourself. This will help you to connect with your quiet core within.

494 **Angel virtues** Bring to mind the virtues of an angel. Then visualize an object or symbol to represent each virtue – for example, a feather for lightness, a gift box for generosity. During the following weeks and months, watch out for these objects appearing in your life. As they do gather them together in a corner of your home, and meditate on them every time you add to the arrangement. When the collection is complete, perform a final meditation and then give them all away.

495 **Special places** Many of us recognize places that allow us more than anywhere else to be ourselves. Be sure that you know such places well, acknowledge their worth, and meditate in them often. Take others there to share their benevolent energies.

496   Make a Zen garden A miniature Zen
garden provides an excellent focus for meditation. To make one
you will require a shallow dish, some sand, and some natural
objects for the "features" (such as stones, leaves or small twigs).
Choose these objects with care, bearing in mind that natural
forms are sacred in Zen. Place the sand in the dish and position
the features in a pleasing formation. Use your fingers to create
wave-like patterns around each object, echoing the way in which
water eddies around rocks and islands. When you meditate on
your Zen garden, notice the paradoxical suggestion of stillness
and movement that this effect creates.

497   Our global home In its widest sense the idea of "home"
refers not just to the place where we live, but also to our planet.
Bring to mind an image of Earth – a small blue and green
planet, orbiting the sun. Feel a sense of love and respect for this
delicate organism on which we are dependent for life. Resolve
to express that love through your daily actions by treating the
planet with the same respect that you accord your home.

Relationships

IN PARTNERSHIP

498   **The ingredients for love**   In its purest form the love we have for our loved one shares the same ingredients as the love we have for our friends.

499   **True life**   "Whoever loves true life, will love true love."
ELIZABETH BARRETT BROWNING (1806–1861)

500   **The wellspring of love**   To love and be loved we must allow ourselves to be vulnerable.

501   **Open to love**   Imagine yourself as a flowerbud, head bowed, petals tightly furled. Gradually you become pleasantly aware of a warm tingle as the morning sun strikes the base of your petals. You lift your head and loosen your petals a little. As the sunlight gets warmer, you feel encouraged to open further until your exquisite petals, delicate hues and intoxicating scent are revealed in all their glory. In the same way, allow the warmth of your partner's love to open your heart, allowing its full beauty to be revealed.

502 **Our most difficult task** "For one human being to love another: that is perhaps the most difficult of all our tasks, the ultimate, the last test and proof, the work for which all other work is but preparation." RAINER MARIA RILKE (1875–1926)

503 **Send out love** This meditation will help you to feel and express your love for another person. Close your eyes and meditate on the word "love". How does it appear in your mind's eye? Note the hues it is written in and whether it is glowing or sparkling. How does your body respond to the word? Do you feel a warmth or tingling? Bring to mind the person to whom you would like to express your feelings. Imagine them cocooned in your love. Notice how happy and safe this makes them feel. Resolve to express these feelings of love to the person next time you see them, whether through words, gestures or simply your presence.

504   **Eye to eye** When was the last time you looked properly into your partner's eyes? Conjure those eyes now, in your mind – their tint, their shape, the person who lives deep in the well of their pupils. Spend five minutes or so dwelling on this image, with love. Then go and find your partner: do it for real.

505   **Touching palms** During their first meeting Juliet tells Romeo: "Saints have hands that pilgrim's hands do touch,/ And palm to palm is holy palmers' kiss" (I.5 *Romeo and Juliet* by Shakespeare). In these words she reminds us of the sacred element in intimate relationships. To heighten this sense of the sacred, bring mindfulness (present-moment awareness) to each of the daily interactions between you and your partner. With this attitude even small intimacies, such as doing the dishes together, present opportunities for deepening your connection.

506 **Summer leaves** "We've touched a thousand ways, like summer leaves touching." CHINESE POEM

507 **Capture an intimate moment** Intimacy nourishes the soul of a relationship. Yet in long-term cohabiting relationships, it is all too easy for intimacy to disappear amid the mundane concerns of daily life. Bring to mind one of the most intimate moments in your relationship. Recapture the positive feelings

of warmth, love, openness and trust that you experienced in that moment and meditate on them. Expanding these feelings within the present moment will help to nurture them within your relationship as it is now.

508 The consciousness of love "The consciousness of loving and being loved brings a warmth and a richness to life that nothing else can bring." OSCAR WILDE (1854–1900)

509 The beauty of a snowflake A harmonious relationship is as beautiful as a snowflake. When snow of such beauty descends, why stay inside?

510 Perfect love "Love is infallible; it has not errors, for all errors are the want of love." ANDREW BONAR LAW (1858–1923)

511 May-pole dancing In the Celtic tradition, the special time for lovers is the festival of Beltane on May Day. On this occasion lovers hold hands around the May pole while dancers bind them

together with ribbons tied to the top of the pole. Imagine you
and your partner standing beneath a May pole. You are
surrounded by dancers, who weave in and out, binding you
together with rainbow-tinted ribbons. As the ribbons tighten feel
the love between you and your partner grow ever stronger.

512 **Evergreen love** Meditate on the evergreen tree as a symbol
for the constancy of your love. Visualize an evergreen standing
in the midst of a forest of deciduous trees. As autumn arrives,
watch the other trees lose their leaves, while the evergreen
remains green. Practise this meditation to help sustain the love
in your relationship through good times and bad.

513 **A pair of swans** Pairing for life at four years of age, swans
provide the perfect metaphor for eternal love. Meditate on the
image of two swans, gliding gracefully together across calm
waters or soaring through clouds. Absorb the peace and harmony
that exist between the swans. Imagine your relationship imbued
with the spirit of these qualities. Now make this vision real.

514 **Mutual ties** A hook is one-sided: it is thrown by one party into the relationship. A bond is mutual: it is a knot that both parties cherish. Let us banish our hooks and tighten our bonds.

515 **Wild places** "The mind I love must have wild places, a tangled orchard where dark damsons drop in the heavy grass, an overgrown little wood, the chances of a snake or two, a pool that no body's fathomed the depth of, and paths threaded with flowers planted by the mind." KATHERINE MANSFIELD (1888–1923)

516 **The eternal ring** In many societies marriage is one of life's most significant rites of passage, an affirmation of continuing order on both the human and cosmic scale. It symbolizes a binding union between two opposite principles, male and female, seen as necessary to create and protect new life. Among the unifying symbols still used at weddings is the ring, an emblem of the indivisible and eternal. Meditate on your 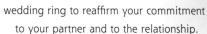 wedding ring to reaffirm your commitment to your partner and to the relationship.

517 **The wholeness of love** "Just as I love my village with a part of my love from my country, so I love my love with a part of my love for the One." MODERN AFFIRMATION

518 **A skilled performance** Visualize yourself as a performer on stage, with your loved one as the audience. You improvize a creative act bringing all your imagination and skill to the performance. Imagine your loved one glowing with pleasure. Now bring the same level of skill to your relationship.

519 **Living intimately** When two people live together there is the opportunity for great intimacy. The more deeply you know and love your partner, the more you know and love yourself, and this creates a beneficent double loop that binds you together. To strengthen the bond between you, close your eyes and visualize your mutual love as a double loop of golden light that passes between and around your hearts, endlessly reinforcing itself.

520 **Sharing books** "The pleasure of all reading is doubled when one lives with another who shares the same books." KATHARINE MANSFIELD (1888–1923)

521 **Relationship gardens** "Our relationship is like a gardener's microclimate. If the conditions are right, both of us will grow healthily. I will nurture the ground to the best of my ability." MODERN AFFIRMATION

522 **A perfect chord** "Stand off from me; be still your own;/ Love's perfect chord maintains the sense through harmony, not unison,/ Of finest difference." EDWARD DOWDEN (1843–1913)

523 **Letting go** When you love someone deeply, you may be tempted to place demands and restrictions on them, fearing that they will abandon you. However, if love is to flourish between you, you must give your partner freedom to follow their own path, otherwise they will come to resent you. Visualize your lover as a bird in your hands. Open your hands to release the bird. Watch as the bird flies freely and joyfully in the air above you, before returning to perch on your finger.

524 **Side by side** The Lebanese poet Kahlil Gibran suggests that lovers "Let there be spaces in [their] togetherness." Be like two trees: grow side by side, but not in each others shadow.

525 **Journey into space** As a relationship grows, every so often embark on an imaginary space trip to keep your individuality intact. Close your eyes and visualize yourself as an astronaut. You will be in orbit for a month. You are floating thousands of miles from your loved one, spending nights alone, eating food alone. You feel lonely at times – but you know that this is important work. Get used to the feeling of separation. Next time you see your loved one, you can enjoy a great reunion!

526 **A healing separation** Doubly wounded is the wounded soul that falls in love with its tormenter. Leave and let your wounds be healed.

527 **The joys of meeting** "The joys of meeting pay the pangs of absence; else who could bear it?" NICHOLAS ROWE (1674–1718)

528 **The union of love** "In so far as love is union, it knows no extremes of distance." SOR JUANA INÉS DE LA CRUZ (1651–95)

529 **Love letter** When separated from one you love, conjure up their face as they sit quietly at a desk, thinking of you. Now imagine them writing you a letter. Watch as the words flow onto the page. Visualize what they would write, picking out a few characteristic phrases. Relax in the knowledge of your closeness.

530 **Reunions** "Journeys end in lovers meeting." WILLIAM SHAKESPEARE, *TWELFTH NIGHT*, II.3.

531 **Strands of love** When distance separates you from your partner, visualize strands of love linking your hearts together. An awareness of this connection can give you the strength to bear the separation, knowing that in spirit you are united.

FRIENDSHIP

532 A summons "Friendship runs dancing through the world
bringing to us all the summons to awake and sing its praises."
EPICURUS (C.341–270BCE)

533 Circle of friends Perform this meditation whenever you are
in need of a little extra support. Imagine that you are standing
in the middle of a circle of your dearest friends. They are
looking at you with shining eyes, golden light pouring out of
their hearts toward you. Surrounded by the warmth of their
love, you feel safe and supported, held in a nurturing embrace.

534 Faith When we lose faith in ourselves, it is our friends who
carry it for us until we have strength to hold it for ourselves.

535 Whispers of love If you are feeling lonely, imagine that one
of your dearest friends is by your side. You feel their hand on
your shoulder and hear their voice whispering in your ear. They
are telling you how special you are and that you will always
have a place in their heart. You feel their lips on your forehead

as they kiss you goodbye. You are left with a warm sense of being truly loved for who you are.

536 Revealing our glory
In the warmth of a true friend's love, we can remove the cloak of shame to reveal the full glory of the soul.

537 True friends Like ideal parents, true friends see the beauty of our inner self, loving us regardless of our appearance, foibles

or social position. Secure in their regard we feel free to express the full spectrum of our personality without shyness or inhibition.

538 Thinking aloud "A friend is one before whom I may think aloud." RALPH WALDO EMERSON (1803–1882)

539 Pick a flower for a friend In the summer go to a flower shop or garden and pick a flower for each of your friends. Arrange the flowers in a vase, thinking of your friends as you do so. Now sit and contemplate the arrangement. Meditate on the beauty of the flowers and how they reflect the qualities of your friends. Inwardly acknowledge the benefit that you have received from the positive energies of these friends in your life.

540 Around the fire Close your eyes and imagine gathering around a fire with your closest friends while a blizzard swirls outside. Feel your hands warmed by the fire, your heart by the company. Survey the glowing faces around you and appreciate their beauty, each one unique as a snowflake or fingerprint.

541   **Play a signature tune** Each of us has our own special music
– a particular melody of spirit, character and experience. Choose
a close friend and spend five minutes listening to their signature
tune in your head. Finish this meditation with an inward round
of applause for everything this friend brings to your life.

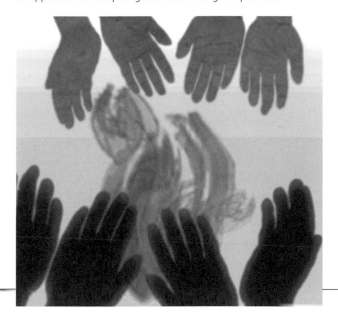

542 **One soul, two bodies** "What is a friend? A single soul dwelling in two bodies." ARISTOTLE (384–322BCE)

543 **Letter of love** Close your eyes and bring to mind one of your dearest friends. Imagine writing a letter in which you tell them of the many things that you love about them. Visualize the expression on their face when they read the letter, which confirms how special they are to you. Now do this for real.

544 **Silent exchanges** "If friendship is firmly established between two hearts, they do not need to exchange news." SA'IB OF TABRIZ (C.1601–1677)

545 **Visualize a blessing** Sit opposite a friend, cup your hands and hold them beneath your heart. Imagine the white sparkling light of a blessing flowing out of your heart into your hands. Reach out and pour the blessing over the crown of the other person's head. Trace with your hands the outline of their head as you imagine your blessing flowing into their body.

546 **Ritual of giving** Treat wrapping a gift as a meditation on
the friend for whom it is destined. As you fold the paper over
the gift, imagine that you are wrapping your friend in the
embrace of your love.

547 **Friendship's bounty** "If we have wealth but no friends, we
will never be happy. If we have friends, we will be happy, even
without wealth." EPICURUS (C.341–270BCE)

548 **Befriend yourself** To build real friendships with others
we must first make friends with ourselves. Close your eyes and
imagine meeting yourself for the first time. Engage yourself
in conversation: share your fears and concerns, your hopes
and dreams; show compassion for your feelings. Conclude with
a gesture of appreciation and promise to meet again soon.

549 **Heart song** "A friend is someone who knows the song in
your heart and can sing it back to you when you have forgotten
the words." ANONYMOUS

MAKING CONNECTIONS

550 **Listening** "Listen, or your tongue will keep you deaf."
NATIVE AMERICAN PROVERB

551 **The eel and the salmon** The eel and the salmon cross each other on their opposite journeys across the Atlantic, travelling thousands of miles to breed. Our purposes may be no less different from each other, but when we meet, let us spend time together and share our insights.

552 **Truth-telling** "It is very hard to say the exact truth, even about your own immediate feelings – much harder than to say something fine about them which is not the exact truth."
GEORGE ELIOT (1819–80)

553 **Conversation replay** Reflect on a recent conversation. Visualize the setting in detail and replay the dialogue in your head, recalling body language and tone as well as content. From this detached perspective you may gain a deeper understanding of what the other person communicated to you.

554 **True feeling** "Never apologize for showing feeling. When you do so, you apologize for the truth." Benjamin Disraeli (1804–1881)

555 **Sharing silence** Meditating with other people can deepen your relationship. Sit in a circle, in silence together. Close your eyes and, as a group, meditate on the sense of separateness and connection between you.

556 **Offerings of love** "He who offers to me with devotion only a leaf, or a flower, or a fruit, or even a little water, this I accept from that yearning soul, because with a pure heart it was offered with love." Bhagavad Gita (1st or 2nd century)

557 **The magic circle** Any conversation creates a circle of trust. Next time you are talking to someone, in the pauses relish this trust flowing round in a perfect system. It is one of life's gifts.

558 **True giving** "I will not be hurt if my gift is undervalued: when I give, I expect nothing in return." Modern affirmation

559 **The richness of generosity** "From the infinitely changeless vessel of spirit, I savour the inexhaustible richness of generosity." EDUARDO CUADRA (1820–1903)

560 **Sharing, giving, loving** Take stock of what you have to give others – whether practical or emotional, constructive or empathetic. As long as we are ready to give, to share and to love when the time comes, we have a purpose. And with such a purpose we can never be lost or alone.

561 **The gift of the self** "The only gift is a portion of thyself." RALPH WALDO EMERSON (1803–1882)

562 **Opening the door** "The door to the human heart can be opened only from the inside." SPANISH PROVERB

563 **Heartfelt invitation** If you find it difficult to open your heart to someone, close your eyes and imagine them knocking at the door of your heart. Open the door and welcome them in.

564 **Loving reflections** Sustained, loving relationships are
essential to psychological well-being. Reflected in the eyes
of others – seen and understood – we affirm our existence.

565 **The frozen mask** We need not worry if we cannot cry: all
gentle souls will see our pain even when numbness masks it.

BRIDGING THE GAP

566 **Entertaining angels** "Let brotherly love continue. Be not forgetful to entertain strangers: for thereby some have entertained angels unawares." HEBREWS 13.2

567 **A bridge to an island** Imagine yourself as a floating island. Around you are other islands – all the people whose lives come close to yours, by choice or by chance. Pick an island that has only recently swum into view. Imagine throwing out a bridge and walking over to this new land. Who is the person? What is the bridge? Answer these questions. Make your connection.

568 **Mirror, mirror** On some level, everybody we meet serves as a mirror to us. Often the traits we are repelled by in others are traits that we are secretly ashamed of in ourselves; similarly, the qualities we admire in others are ones that we too possess but may not have acknowledged within ourselves.

569 **A change of focus** To change a relationship, we must change ourselves, not the other person.

570   **Find the teacher in everyone** Approach people with
curiosity: everybody has something they can teach you. Spend
some time thinking about the various people you encountered
today, particularly those whom you disliked or whose ideas or
opinions you disagreed with. What can you find of value in
what they have done or said? Inwardly acknowledge gratitude
for the teachings of these individuals.

571   **Dissolving emnity** Whenever someone hurts or angers you,
practise this meditation to bring compassion to the situation. In
your mind conjure up the other person. What was it about their
actions that caused you distress? Try to understand why they
behaved the way they did. Can you think of times in your own
life when you have done something similar? Recall how you felt
at that time and why you behaved in that way. From this
perspective you may begin to see the other person not as
fundamentally flawed, but as a fellow human being caught in
a bad moment. As you soften to them, notice if your perception
of the situation alters, becoming less black and white. With the

other person no longer cast in the role of villain, you may be able to appreciate more clearly your own part in the drama.

572 Understanding "Do not weep; do not wax indignant. Understand." BARUCH SPINOZA (1632–77)

573 The strength to forgive "The weak can never forgive. Forgiveness is the attribute of the strong." MAHATMA GANDHI (1869–1948)

574 Breaking the arrows of hurt Sometimes out of tiredness or hurt, we react to others in anger, firing arrows into their heart. Regretting our reaction we then fire arrows at ourselves. When this occurs close your eyes and imagine plucking out the arrows you have fired and breaking them in half. Now visualize the healing light of forgiveness around the two wounded hearts.

575 Making amends Visualize reconciling your differences with someone you have had a falling out with. Imagine sharing a positive experience with them, such as a walk in the park. This will help you to think of them as a friend, so that you encounter them in the happy memory of shared enjoyment.

576 Understanding others Building a relationship means understanding the needs and feelings of another person. Use meditation to help you listen to and fully hear other people by focusing on stilling your mind and opening your heart. Undistracted by your own feelings and concerns, you will find it easier to give others your full attention and to hold their needs and feelings in your heart with compassion and acceptance.

577 Healing words We walk among others with a cure that could heal many ills, so why don't we use it more often? All we need to do is say: "I was wrong. I am sorry. Please forgive me."

578 Think before you speak "Before you speak, ask yourself: is it kind, is it necessary, is it true, does it improve on the silence?" SHIRDI SAI BABA (1856–1918)

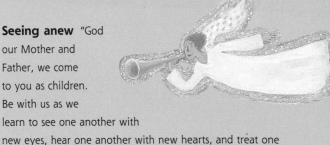

579   **Seeing anew** "God our Mother and Father, we come to you as children. Be with us as we learn to see one another with new eyes, hear one another with new hearts, and treat one another in a new way." CORRYMEELA COMMUNITY (20TH CENTURY)

580   **Clearing the air** Practise this meditation after an argument. Close your eyes and imagine observing a storm through your bedroom window. Wind whips the trees and rain beats down on the earth. Streaks of lightning rip through the clouds, followed by terrifying thunderclaps. Watching the storm you feel completely calm, knowing that you are safe in your home. Gradually, the storm abates and the world becomes quiet. The dark clouds part and a shaft of sunlight penetrates the gloom. In a tree by your window, a bird begins to sing. You feel joyful and at peace, ready to enter the world once again.

Happiness

EVERYDAY CONTENTMENT

581   **The absence of striving** "Happiness is the absence of striving for happiness." CHUANG TZU (c.369–286BCE)

582   **The art of being** Contentment comes from neither doing nor having, but from being.

583   **Twin sisters** The German philosopher Friedrich Nietzsche understood pain as the flip side of pleasure. He likened the two to twin sisters that grow up together or remain small together. If we seek only to protect ourselves from pain, we limit our capacity for joy; if we embrace pain as an inevitable part of living, we open ourselves up to greater fulfilment.

584   **Being without** "To be without some of the things you want is an indispensable part of happiness." BERTRAND RUSSELL (1872–1970)

585   **Cultivate contentment** This meditation expands our capacity to derive contentment from the simple pleasures of life. **1** Close your eyes and consider the word "contentment". What does it mean to you? How does it manifest itself in your thoughts and feelings? **2** Recall a time in the past when you felt contented –

perhaps while playing ball in the garden or spending time with loved ones. Imagine yourself in that moment now, allowing the feelings of contentment to fill your mind and body. **3** Now bring that sense of contentment into the present moment.

586 **The inscrutable** "The quiet solitary person apprehends the inscrutable – seeking nothing, holding to the middle way, and remaining free from attachments." I CHING (12TH CENTURY BCE)

587 **Consider the snake** In an old folktale a snake was once asked whether it would have preferred to have legs, if given the choice. The snake was mystified by the question. "No," it said, "I am what I am." We are what we are. We need have no wish for anything that we do not have.

588 **Finding balance** Take a pencil and draw a wheel made up of six segments representing important areas of your life: work, relationships, family, health, spirituality and creativity. Proportion the size of each segment according to the contribution it makes to your sense of self. Now use the wheel as a mandala in a meditation. Perceive it not as a collection of parts, but as a wholeness – a patterned circle. Let the image rest in your mind without judgment. The centre reflects your indivisible self.

589 **Ways to live** "In dwelling, live close to the ground. In thinking, keep to the simple. In conflict, be fair and generous. In governing, don't try to control. In work, do what you enjoy. In family life, be completely present." LAO TZU (C.604–531BCE)

590 **A moment's rest** "Rest is not idleness, and to lie sometimes on the grass on a summer day listening to the murmur of water or watching the clouds float across the sky, is hardly a waste of time." SIR J. LUBBOCK (1834–1913)

591 **A still pond** According to Chinese philosophy, action and contemplation are the attributes of the King and the Sage respectively, representing the two key aspects of a balanced life. In the West emphasis is often placed on action at the expense of contemplation. If you spend much of your life rushing around, meditate by a still pond or lake. Focus on the calm surface of the water until your mind reflects its stillness.

Alternatively, if you feel lethargic and lacking in motivation, it may be more appropriate to meditate by the running water of a **fountain or stream (592)**. Focus on the lively play of the water, inviting its effervescence to renew your spirit.

593 **Taking time** "Take time to think ... it is the source of power. Take time to play ... it is the secret of perpetual youth. Take time to laugh ... it is the music of the soul. Take time to pray ... it is the greatest power on Earth." Words written on the wall of the Missionaries of Charity children's home, Calcutta, India

594 **Inner smile meditation** Whenever you find yourself in a tough situation, this meditation will give you an instant boost of positive feeling. Imagine that you are looking at your face in a mirror. Watch yourself smile and your eyes light up with joy. Notice how beautiful you look when you smile and appreciate how positive smiling makes you feel. Breathe deeply, bringing that positive feeling to life within you in the present moment.

595 **A moonlit swim** Imagine yourself by a wide river gently flowing through a forest. It is night, and a full moon rises above the trees. You strip off your clothes and swim out into the middle of the river. You float on your back there, looking up at the bright moon, tremendously at peace in this moonlit watery world. The stresses of life are deep in their caves, unable to bear the softness of the moonlight.

596 **True kindness** "Anyone who is truly kind can never be unhappy. Anyone who is truly wise can never be muddled." CONFUCIUS (551–479BCE)

597 **Your best-loved place** Close your eyes and imagine yourself in your best-loved place. Visualize the setting in as much detail as possible, conjuring up smells and sounds as well as sights. Remember the positive feelings evoked by the place and bring those feelings back with you into the present.

598 **Garden of the mind** Visualize yourself in a garden. The overgrown foliage of discontent blocks out the light and the weeds of worry choke the path. Armed with a fork and pruning shears you begin digging up the weeds and cutting back the shrubs. Penetrating deeper into the garden, you discover features previously unknown to you – a well of love and a fountain of creativity. Having cleared the soil you plant the seeds of joy and laughter. Each day you tend your plants, watching as your flowers of contentment come into bloom.

599 **Sunshine** "Those who bring sunshine into the lives of others, cannot keep it from themselves." JAMES M. BARRIE (1860–1937)

600 **A tropical paradise**
For many people a holiday on a tropical island offers the ultimate escape from the stresses of daily life. Yet we can conjure up a tropical paradise wherever we are. Close your eyes and take a few deep breaths. Imagine reclining in

a hammock on a tropical beach. Feel the warmth of the sun and the caress of the sea breeze. Allow your breathing to synchronize with the rhythmic crashing of the surf along the beach. Feel tension release from your body each time you exhale.

601 **The golden thread** Even the quietest kind of happiness has passion for life running through it like a golden thread. Trace that thread within yourself. It is endless. It is your spiritual bloodstream. Trace its endless glowing path in your mind's eye.

602 **The process of happiness** "Happiness is a process, not a destination. So work like you don't need the money. Love like you've never been hurt. And dance as though no one is watching." ANONYMOUS

603 **Sacred lives** In the Native American tradition, the sacred and the everyday are not opposites. Even the most ordinary acts of daily life are imbued with deep meaning and significance – an attitude that breeds quiet contentment. We can cultivate this attitude within ourselves by giving full attention to everything we do; in doing so we assert the sacredness of our lives.

604 **Peacock feathers** When we look at peacock feathers from certain angles, their iridescent blues and greens shimmer with beauty. Many things in life reveal their intrinsic qualities when perceived in the right way, but often familiarity dulls our responses, making their beauty difficult to see. Look at the things around you with fresh eyes, seeing them as if for the first time. You'll find riches you never imagined.

605 **Open the window** "Each day I open the window of my world, bringing in light to flood me with hope, fresh air to fill me with joy and new vistas to expand my horizons." MODERN AFFIRMATION

606 **The Japanese crane** In Japan the crane is a symbol of happiness and prosperity. Meditate on the image of the crane. The white of its black-and-white feathers represents purity; the red spot on its head, associated with fire, represents vitality.

607   A moment of alchemy
"Every moment lived fully is a moment of transcendent alchemy, of fire transforming dull metals to dazzling gold." ANONYMOUS

608   Just be If we are not careful, meditation can become just one more thing that we think we need to do to improve ourselves – an attitude typical of our perfectionist culture. In fact, true peace comes from being at one with how we are right now, rather than with some ideal person that we hope to be in the future.

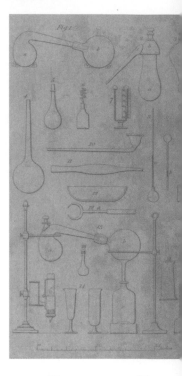

If we view meditation as a process without a clearly defined outcome, we create a space in which to sit with ourselves, quietly observing our thoughts and feelings, allowing ourselves to be.

609 **Hermit power** This visualization will put you in touch with a more contemplative way of living – an antidote to the action-oriented culture of Western society. Imagine that you are living like a hermit in a cave. Completely alone, free from the demands and restrictions imposed by work, family, relationships and the rest of the outside world, there is little to distract you from the present moment. Whether you are tending to your basic needs for food, warmth and cleanliness, or engaged in quiet contemplation, you are completely present with yourself – able to appreciate the joy of simply being alive. How would it feel to live such an life? Consider how you can bring some of the benefits of hermit-living into your everyday routine.

610 **The way to heaven** "All the way to heaven is heaven."
St Catherine of Siena (1347–80)

611 **Letting be** Much of the discord we experience comes from resisting what is. Take a step toward inner harmony by accepting whatever is happening in the moment. Silently say "yes" to your thoughts and feelings, the sensations within your body, and the sights and sounds that you see and hear around you. Once you allow what is to simply be there, without wishing to change it in any way, you make contact with the stillness at the heart of being.

612 **The truth of the moment** During meditation ask yourself: "What is the truest statement I could make about myself now?" Write the statement down and meditate upon it for a while. As you sit with it, notice what feelings it elicits. Then ask if there is a truer statement you could make about yourself. Repeat this process until you feel that you have come as close as possible to the truth of your experience in the moment.

613 **Candle meditation** This is a simple meditation – perfect for the beginner. In a dark room sit on the floor with a lighted

candle in front of you. Gaze at the flame
through half-closed eyes for a few moments.
Then close your eyes and focus on the
after-glow of the flame behind your eyelids.
Allow the light to fill your mind. If you find
that your attention drifts, open your eyes
a little and look at the flame. Then close
your eyes again when you feel ready.
Continue for as long as feels comfortable.

614 **Complete presence** Practise mindfulness by spending ten
minutes consciously trying to be fully aware of the rich and
complex sensory experience of each moment – appreciate the
shapes and hues of all you see, the sounds and smells around
you and the touch of air and fabric against your skin. You may
find that your mind tries to resist such discipline by sliding out
of the present moment into the past or future. When this occurs,
simply bring your mind back to the present moment. It is from
here that we catch glimpses of bliss.

615 The sound of silence Sit in a quiet place, close your eyes and focus on listening to the sounds around you. As you do so you may find that noises you might otherwise have missed begin to emerge from the silence – perhaps the sighing of the wind, the trilling of birdsong, the beating of your heart. Gradually shift your focus to the silence between the sounds. Allow a deeper stillness to permeate your consciousness.

616 Regret-free zone Meditate on the space in your mind where regrets would dwell, if you had them. That space is empty. You regret nothing that you have done and nothing that you have left undone. You could have seen more by lifting your eyes higher, but even this you do not regret. Free from all regrets, you are happy.

617 Look to this day "Dreams of yesterday whisper to me; visions of tomorrow beckon. Yet it is today where I must live, here where the current of life quickens my blood, electrifying each moment." ADAPTED FROM KALIDASA, INDIAN PLAYWRIGHT (5TH CENTURY)

618   **The moment's flowering** "Artist, poet or teacher – if you want to fix and immortalize your ideas or your feelings, seize them at the precise and fleeting moment, for it is their highest moment." AMIEL (D.1881)

619   **Dissolving anchors** As we go about our daily business, our energies often become scattered. While anticipating what the day holds, we may also think about the past or future – perhaps some recent triumph, an action that we regret, or a future conversation. These attachments to other times leach your energy and distract your attention from your experience in the moment. Visualize these attachments as anchors, which are weighing you down. Now imagine these anchors dissolving away, freeing you to be fully conscious of the present.

620   **Awaiting the butterfly** "Happiness is a butterfly, which, when pursued, is always just beyond your grasp, but which, if you will sit down quietly, may alight upon you." NATHANIEL HAWTHORNE (1804–1864)

621 **Fully present** "I am fully present for whatever and whomever I encounter. I respond sensitively to any situations that may arise." MODERN AFFIRMATION

622 **Cook mindfully** Rather than viewing cooking as a chore, treat it as an opportunity to practise the meditative technique of mindfulness, or full alertness to the present moment. You will find that it makes cooking more enjoyable and enriching. As you prepare and cook the food, feast your senses on the hues, shapes, textures and smells of the ingredients – for example, the rich burgundy sheen of an eggplant, the honeyed perfume of a melon. Perform each action with deliberation and care as though partaking in a ritual act. Before serving the meal, give thanks for the food and the presence of the guests with whom you will share it.

623 **Be where you are** "As you walk and eat and travel, be where you are. Otherwise you will miss most of your life." THE BUDDHA (C.563–C.460BCE)

624 **Rediscovering the world** An unusual way to cultivate a heightened awareness of the present moment is to explore nature blindfolded with the help of a partner. Working in silence, take it in turns to guide each other around a garden, park or other natural setting. As the sighted partner, assist the blindfolded partner in exploring the simple delights of nature – perhaps the delicate scent of a flower, the knobbled bark of a tree or the sharp sweetness of a blackberry. In the absence of sight or sound, the blindfolded partner learns to surrender to the present moment, enjoying the intimacy of each experience as it unfolds.

625 **Fleeting joy** "He who binds to himself a joy/ Does the wingéd life destroy;/ But he who kisses the joy as it flies/ Lives in eternity's sun rise." WILLIAM BLAKE (1757–1827)

626 **Open your eyes** "I open my eyes to the wonder of being. Delighted at the way my life turns out, amazed at the beauty of it all, I am happy." MODERN AFFIRMATION

THE JOY OF PLAY

627   **Inner harmony** "I am at play in the world. Everything that I experience fills me with delight. My greatest pleasure lies in sharing and spreading joy." MODERN AFFIRMATION

628   **A moment's rest** "The creation of something new is not accomplished by the intellect but by the play instinct acting from inner necessity. The creative mind plays with the objects it loves." CARL JUNG (1875–1961)

629   **Focus on happy memories** Practise this meditation to reconnect with your natural state of joy in times of stress. Find a picture of yourself laughing as a child. Study the photograph and allow the positive feelings of the captured moment to seep into your present awareness. Try to expand these feelings by visualizing in as much detail as possible the event at which the photograph was taken. Bask in the warmth generated by these happy memories. Now return your focus to the present moment, bringing with you the sense of playfulness and joy that you expressed as a child.

630 The all-embracing game Happiness isn't a spectator sport: all your family and friends get to play too.

631 Play with dolphins The quality of our lives greatly improves when we take time to play. If you find it difficult to let go of your adult inhibitions, imagine swimming with dolphins. Feel the freedom and joy as you join in their games, splashing and diving through the water. Revel in moving exuberantly through the unfamiliar element of the sea.

632 Playing with the wind "And forget not that the earth delights to feel your bare feet and the wind longs to play with your hair." KAHLIL GIBRAN (1883–1931)

633 **Life's playground** As adults we are often solemn about life, worrying endlessly whether we are doing the right thing. But if we view the world as an adventure playground, filled with opportunities for discovery, we will find that many of our anxieties simply fall away. An effective way to overcome fear is to gallop through its ranks in the spirit of exuberance.

634 **The gift of innocence** Although children have limited experience, their appetite and passion for life are boundless. Close your eyes and imagine yourself as a small child. Picture how your world would look from this perspective. Experience a sense of wonder at everything you see around you. Returning to your current self, see if you can fuse this freshness of vision with the maturity that you have gained as an adult.

635 **Lifting the burden** "How refreshing to hear the whinny of a packhorse when its burden is lifted off its back!" ZEN SAYING

636 **The explorer** "The places I visit, the people I meet and the ideas I encounter make me an explorer – a Columbus of the spirit, breaking new ground every day." MODERN AFFIRMATION

637 **Exposure** Life is full of exhilarating risks – the risk of meeting, the risk of giving, the risk of loving. We must throw ourselves into these risks with all our hearts. We cannot be whole without exposure. We cannot be happy standing still.

GRATITUDE

638   **Parent of virtue** "Gratitude is not only the greatest of virtues, but the parent of all others." CICERO (106–43BCE)

639   **At home in your life** Sit quietly and reflect on your life right now. It is changing. The future is unknown: some of your hopes will not be realized – but neither will some of your fears. Also, you are getting older. You are on a journey, moving in a landscape that itself is in constant flux. All these changes constitute "home". Take a few minutes to appreciate where you are now in your life ... and feel grateful for it.

640   **Glimpses of eternity** "Giving thanks for the moment is the only way to glimpse eternity." MODERN MEDITATION FROM SPAIN

641   **Silence and appreciation** If we take for granted all the blessings we have – material, mental and spiritual – this is because we cannot imagine ourselves without them any more than we can imagine ourselves never talking. In your meditations, be silent. Cherish what you have.

642 **The world's cooperation** "Give thanks for everything in your world that cooperates to give you life and strength." ST IGNATIUS LOYOLA (1491–1556)

643 **Give thanks** "When you arise in the morning, give thanks for the morning light. Give thanks for your life and your strength. Give thanks for your food and give thanks for the joy of living. And if you see no reason for giving thanks, rest assured that the fault is in yourself." CHIEF TECUMSEH OF THE SHAWNEE NATION (D.1813)

644 **Count your blessings** Gratitude is an outflow of positive energy that responds to an inflow of positive energy. This two-way traffic of blessings and thanks is the equilibrium of a contented life. Nothing is measured and found wanting. We owe our thanks for a thousand blessings, large or small.

645 **Heavenly thanks** "Gratitude is heaven itself."
WILLIAM BLAKE (1757–1827)

646 **Nature's bounty** At mealtimes pay particular attention to
the food that you are eating. Eat slowly, relishing every smell,
taste and texture. Inwardly express gratitude to the earth for
nurturing your body and soul with this meal.

   Share a silent meal with friends (647), together giving full,
grateful attention to the food and the company.

648 **Perfect prayers** "Our single grateful thought raised to
heaven is the most perfect prayer." G. E. LESSING (1729–81)

649 **The privilege of freedom** "On my long walk I am
privileged to be exercising my freedom. Freedom to choose
my route, freedom to decide when to stop, freedom to walk
on without hindrance from others, freedom from ambushes and
landmines, and from the sight of pain and misery – a freedom
precious beyond words." MODERN AFFIRMATION

650   **Celestial joys** "Your enjoyment of the world is never right until every morning you awake in heaven, see yourself in God's palace, and look upon the skies and the Earth and the air as celestial joys, having such a loving regard of all these as if you were among the angels." THOMAS TRAHERNE (1637–74)

651   **Time to move on** Exercising gratitude is a way of achieving closure in a relationship with someone who has departed from your life, but continues to haunt your thoughts. First, bring this person to mind. Review the role that they played in your life and the lessons that they taught you. Imagine thanking them for these lessons and offering them a gift to symbolize your gratitude. Feel the warmth of their gratitude for all that you have given them. After this interaction, see if you experience a sense of completeness that allows you to move on.

652   **Absorb love** Taking the time to appreciate the gifts offered to you by others will help to open your heart to the giving and receiving of love. Begin by focusing on your heart. Visualize a warm, gentle glow in your chest area and sense the slow, steady rhythm of your heartbeat. As you do so contemplate some of the blessings that other people have brought into your life – perhaps the love of fine art inspired in you by your mother or the empathy shown to you by your best friend. Feel your heart swell with gratitude as you reflect that all these blessings were offered to you in the spirit of love.

653 **Blessings of love** "I open my heart to love, giving thanks for the endless love I am blessed to be able to give and receive." MODERN AFFIRMATION

654 **Open your arms** "God gives nothing to those who keep their arms crossed." BAMBARA (WEST AFRICAN) PROVERB

655 **The scallop shell** The scallop shell is a beautiful sculpted gift from the sea. It symbolizes the feminine principle of receptivity. It is only by remaining open that we will receive and appreciate life's blessings. Receptivity is therefore a magnet for the profound satisfactions available to us all. As you meditate, visualize your spirit opening up like a scallop shell.

656   **Door of the soul** "The soul should always stand ajar, ready to welcome the ecstatic experience." EMILY DICKINSON (1830–86)

657   **Accepting grace** There is sometimes a reluctance to receive because deep down we believe ourselves unworthy. Yet we are all entitled to receive grace (special gifts that we feel we have done nothing to deserve) simply by virtue of who and what we are – spiritual beings in human form. Trust in the abundance of the world around you and know your true worthiness. Receive all gifts with joy and gratitude. In doing so you allow the flow of grace to continue as you give back to others the joy you have received.

658   **Dwellings of God** "God has two dwellings: one in heaven, and the other in a meek and thankful heart." IZAAK WALTON (1593–1683)

659   **The transformation of Narcissus** Narcissism is excessive self-absorption, which prevents true connection with others. Paradoxically it is based on a lack of love for the self. The Greek myth of Narcissus indicates how we can resolve this problem. When Narcissus sees his reflection in the water, he sees himself as others see him – as an other. When he falls in love with that other, he not only learns to love himself but he also learns to love others. His transformation into a narcissus flower represents the flowering of his personality when this shift occurs. To overcome our own narcissism we must learn to love ourselves. We can do this by meditating on our reflection in the mirror just as Narcissus meditated on his reflection in the water.

    To take this process deeper, **draw a portrait of yourself (660)**. As you do so try to look at yourself objectively, as an other. Then meditate on the image that you produce.

661   **Strength in weakness** Do not abandon yourself in your weakness. There is strength to be found in embracing the parts of yourself that you dislike.

662 Self to self The relationship at the heart of all our lives is the one we have with ourselves. No other relationship can be an adequate substitute. Regularly spending time in meditation will help you to cultivate this key aspect of your life.

663 **The secret** "Look within! The secret is inside you!"
Hui Neng (638–713)

664 **From judgment to forgiveness** When we judge ourselves
we cut ourselves off from compassion – the energy of the heart.
During your evening meditation acknowledge any self-judgments
you have made during the day and then dissolve them by
uttering the words, "I forgive myself for judging myself." Giving
love to yourself in this way will enable you to reconnect.

665 **Enough as you are** Embedded in our society is an
assumption that who we are is not enough. We are constantly
exhorted to improve ourselves in some way, to become more
beautiful, wealthy, successful or spiritually evolved. A common
response to these messages is to drive ourselves relentlessly in
our efforts to become better people. But what if who we are in
our essential nature is, in fact, enough? What if all we need is to
allow our true beauty to unfold, rather than heroically trying to
change ourselves? Think of yourself as complete, like a seed or

bulb. All you seek lies within – qualities, ideas and states of mind. To live a life of peace, you need nothing more.

666 **Be what you are** "Do not wish to be anything but what you are, and try to be that perfectly." ST FRANCIS DE SALES (1567–1622)

667 **Trees** "Like a tree I stand, reaching for the light, gaining strength from the darkness at my roots. My body is twisted by the storms of life, yet in my uniqueness I am beautiful." MODERN AFFIRMATION

668 **The flowers inside** "Don't go outside to see the flowers. ... Inside your body there are many flowers. One flower has a thousand petals, and that will do for a place to sit. Sitting there you can glimpse the beauty inside the body and out of it, before gardens and after gardens." KABIR (1440–1518)

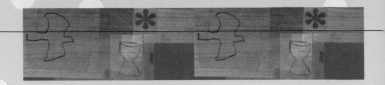

669 **The diamond meditation** Like a diamond the spirit has many facets, which radiate light into the world. Each facet is an essential quality – for example, love, peace, compassion, acceptance and patience. During the course of a week, choose one essential quality each morning and meditate upon it, allowing it to shape your consciousness. Each evening reflect on how that facet of your spirit expressed itself during the day.

670 **Be your own best friend** We often judge ourselves much more harshly than we judge our friends. Yet when we are loving toward ourselves, we flower into the essentially compassionate beings that we really are. Close your eyes and imagine that you are your own best friend – a warm, caring person who sees you and thinks of you in a loving and supportive way. Acknowledge your good qualities to yourself and praise your recent successes, no matter how small. To finish, give yourself a hug. Enjoy the feeling of being truly loved for who you are.

671 An invincible summer "In the depths of the winter I finally found in myself an invincible summer." ALBERT CAMUS (1913–60)

672 Value yourself Many of us tend to think that the things we dislike about ourselves cancel out our positive qualities, rendering us fundamentally flawed. A more loving approach is to view our positive qualities as reflections of our true selves, and our defects as arising out of alienation from our true selves – perhaps because we are in a state of fear. When we value our positive qualities, we come into alignment with our true selves. This enables us to express those qualities more fully, becoming more truly who we are. What are your true qualities? Look inside yourself and rejoice in your virtues.

If you find it hard to think of such qualities, **recall the compliments (673)** that people have given you over the years, or **ask a friend (674)** to describe the qualities they see in you.

675 The wonders within "We carry within us the wonders we seek without us." SIR THOMAS BROWNE (1605–1682)

676 **The treasure chest** Reflect on the treasure that lies within you – gifts such as love, strength, courage and empathy. Make a point of focusing on these positive qualities; learn to trust all you have and all you are. As you do so your inner treasure chest will open, revealing your gifts to everyone around you.

677 **Delight in the self** "Taking delight in our own special kind of action, each one of us attains perfection." *Bhagavad Gita* (1st or 2nd century)

678 **Heart song of praise** Imagine that, as you go through your day, your heart spends all its time singing your praises. The frequency of the song is too high for you to hear. But even when you think that others may have doubts about your qualities, you can take reassurance from the knowledge of this perpetual appreciation. Within yourself you know your worth.

679 **Expansion** "Your playing small doesn't serve you. There is nothing enlightened about shrinking." Nelson Mandela (b.1918)

680   The visiting hero Close your eyes and picture yourself walking around your local town. Imagine that you are a mythic hero on an important mission. You are special, although everyone who sees you thinks that you are just like them. You take pleasure in your secret goal and pride in your ability to fulfil your purpose. Enumerate your special qualities and feel joy swell your heart.

681   Fill your own cup When the demands of life seem overwhelming, it is easy to neglect ourselves. Yet if we omit to fill our own cup we will have nothing left for others. Take a few minutes each day to nurture yourself. To do this first imagine yourself as an empty goblet. Now visualize a pitcher filling up the goblet until it is overflowing with the golden elixir of love. You now have an abundance of love to give to others.

DEALING WITH TROUBLES

682   **Tune the radio**   This meditation helps us to clear anxieties from our minds. Sit comfortably and focus on any feelings of unease. Tune in to one of these feelings as you would into a radio channel. Once aware of a distinct feeling, either do something about it or let it go. Continue tuning into any other anxieties. Having identified and released all of them, tune into the silence, allowing it to fill your mind.

683   **Zen awareness**   "Live with a Zen awareness and no more worries about not being perfect." SENG TSAN (c.520–606)

684   **Beekeeping**   If you are being disturbed by the constant hum of anxieties, close your eyes and visualize these troubles as a swarm of bees buzzing around your head. In your mind conjure up a beehive in front of you. Mentally guide the bees one by one into the hive. As the last ones disappear from sight, the buzzing ceases. Your anxieties have been shepherded away to a place where they cannot bother you.

685 **Defeat the dragon**
If you feel plagued by
worry, close your eyes
and visualize it in the
form of a dragon.
Imagine pursuing the
dragon with a sword.
Battle with it heroically
until it retreats into its
lair. Empowered by
your ability to drive

away the worry, you now feel ready to tackle the cause of
the dragon's wrath – the source of your concerns.

686 **Dandelion clock** Close your eyes and imagine holding a
white, fluffy dandelion. The fluffy seeds represent the stresses
currently on your mind. Begin to blow them away. As you do
so imagine your stresses carried away with each breath. How
many "dandelion hours" does it take to calm your mind?

687   **Lighten your load** When negative thoughts weigh you down, imagine each thought turning into a bubble in your mind and floating out of the top of your head. Feel tension floating away with the bubbles, leaving your spirit and mind lighter.

688   **Facing the sun** "Turn your face to the sun and the shadows fall behind you." MAORI PROVERB

689   **Taming the animals** The Greek hero Orpheus could tame animals by playing his lyre and singing. We can tame our anxieties in the same way. Choose a beautiful piece of music and, as you listen to it, visualize your worries as animals being gradually soothed by the music. By the end of the piece they are lying peacefully by your feet and you feel much calmer.

Get to know this music well and **bring the piece to mind (690)** to calm you whenever you are feeling anxious.

691   **Focus on birdsong** Sitting comfortably, close your eyes and spend a few moments tuning into the chatter of anxieties that are disrupting your inner calm. Imagine these thoughts as the cacophony of jungle sounds – monkeys screeching, elephants trumpeting and so on. Imagine that above the din you detect the beautiful, soaring notes of a songbird. Focus on the bird's singing. As you do so notice how the other jungle sounds fade into the background, leaving you with a sense of peace.

692 **Humming bee breath** The humming sound produced during this breathing exercise creates a vibration in the body that is very nurturing, helping to calm the nerves. Sit comfortably with your eyes closed. Focus your attention on your breath and take a long inhalation. As you exhale, hum gently with your mouth closed but your jaw relaxed. Repeat for eight to twelve more breaths, humming on each exhalation. Allow the sound to vibrate all through your face and head.

693 **Bask in sunlight** "Do not anticipate trouble, or worry about what may never happen. Keep in the sunlight."
BENJAMIN FRANKLIN (1706–1790)

The wider world

CONNECTING WITH NATURE

694 **Sacred lights** Meditating on the wonders of nature can bring us into contact with the spiritual. Close your eyes and visualize the *Aurora Borealis*, or Northern lights. These are the shimmering lights that can sometimes be observed in the sky in the northernmost latitudes. As you imagine the delicate veils of light falling across the night, feel your spirit stir as it recognizes its own beauty in their coruscating illuminations.

695 **The lessons of stones** "Nature teaches more than she preaches. There are no sermons in stones. It is easier to get a spark out of a stone than a moral." JOHN BURROUGHS (1837–1921)

696 **Walking on water** Living by the waterways of Central and South America is a fascinating creature called the basilisk, nicknamed the Jesus Christ lizard because of its remarkable ability to run across water. Visualize this creature with its large, webbed hind feet, running across the surface of a pond. Take a moment to marvel at this miracle of nature and resolve to remain open to and revere the miraculous wherever you go.

697 The nature of miracles "Miracles do not happen in contradiction to nature, but only in contradiction to that which is known to us of nature." St Augustine (354–430ce)

698 Moon shadow Meditate on your moon shadow. Imagine yourself walking through a landscape of fields and woods in the magic light of a full moon. See your moon shadow walk beside you on the hedgerows and bushes, and behind you on the hillsides. This is the light beyond reason – enough to see by when the sun of reason has given us all the daylight it can.

699 The marvellous "In all things of nature there is something of the marvellous." Aristotle (384–322bce)

700 Order amid chaos On a clear night, meditate on the stars. See if you can identify constellations, such as Orion and Taurus. As you trace the patterns of the stars, feel reassured by the order that exists amid apparent chaos. Now meditate on the patterns that exist within yourself, belying a mass of contradictions.

701 **The forces of nature** The random upheavals of nature remind us of all that we are powerless to change – all that we must accept in our lives and in the world around us. In your mind's eye visualize yourself gazing with awe at an earthquake, volcano or hurricane. As you do so acknowledge and accept the invincible forces of nature – and reflect with compassion on those whose lives are overturned by them.

702 **By design** "By forces seemingly antagonistic and destructive, Nature accomplishes her beneficent designs – now a flood of fire, now a flood of ice, now a flood of water, and again, in the fullness of time, an outburst of organic life." John Muir (1838–1914)

703 **Nature's majesty** I surrender to the majesty of nature – the indiscriminate rage of the storm, the impassive resolve of the mountain, the inconstant promise of the moon.

704 **A cloak of protection** "As I travel through the night, protect me with a cloak of Heaven's shining might, moon's floating light, fire's passionate flare, ocean's swirling depth, earth's grounding patience, wind's soaring wildness, owl's piercing eyesight." ADAPTED FROM AN ICELANDIC PRAYER

705 **Elemental gifts** The sages of antiquity believed that the four elements – fire, earth, water and air – were energy forces that sustained the world. Meditate on the profound power of the elements and the enormity of their combined force. Close with a prayer of thanksgiving for all that the elements give us.

  Each element of nature has qualities which reflect the qualities of spirit. Meditate on each individual element to remind you of your own spiritual qualities. **Air (706)** is associated with purity, connection and the invisible life-force. The flowing energy of

water (707) is cleansing and life-sustaining and is associated with knowledge. **Earth (708)** has a solid and stable energy that is nurturing and nourishing. **Fire (709)** is associated with purification, passion and liberation.

710 The goodness of water "The highest good is like that of the water. The goodness of water is that it benefits the ten thousand creatures, yet itself does not scramble, but is content with the places that all men disdain." LAO TZU (C.604–531BCE)

711 Caring for plants Transform the tasks of tending to your plants into meditative activities. As you water them feed them or protect them from winter frosts, feel the warmth of love in your heart for these precious living organisms which provide the oxygen we need to breathe.

712 Undiscovered virtues "What is a weed? A plant whose virtues have not yet been discovered." RALPH WALDO EMERSON (1803–1882)

713 **Faith in nature** The earth, and all its trees and plants, feel loved by our touch and by our gaze. Let us not betray this love. Let us stay true to our faith in nature.

714 **Earth energy** Collect a handful of pebbles in your hand and lightly play with them. Feel their smoothness and listen to the sound they make as they click against each other. Imagine the earth they have been lying in for so many years. Tap into the vast powers that created our planet.

715 **Embrace the earth** This is an enjoyable way to connect with the earth as a living entity. Lie face down on a patch of grass with your arms outstretched as though embracing the earth. Appreciate its support as it holds your body, safe and secure. Tune into the vibrations of energy that pulse through the soil, connecting you in a bond of love.

716 The dance of time "I take into my heart the gentle rhythms of nature performing its perennial dance of time." MODERN AFFIRMATION

717 Be a rock Sit quietly with closed eyes. Bring to mind a life form or other aspect of nature, such as a bird, tree, waterfall or rock. Become this thing in your imagination. Feel its presence; sense what it's like to be in its body, to live its life. How is it being treated by humans? What does it require to thrive? What wisdom – and warnings – does it have for us? Jot down the answers for reflection later on.

718 Sole connections "Healthy feet can hear the very heart of the Holy Earth." CHIEF SITTING BULL (1831–90)

719 Reconnect with nature Time spent in nature is healing. It grounds us in our bodies and reaffirms our felt connection with the world around us. Spend time in green spaces as often as you can, whether in gardens, parks or open countryside. Engage each of your senses in the experience of being at one with nature. Notice the shapes and hues of the flowers, hear the singing of the birds, smell the earthy scents of the ground and the fragrance of flowers.

We can also reconnect to nature using the imagination. Close your eyes and **visualize a meadow (720)** on a sunny afternoon. Notice different species of plants, birds, animals and insects. Watch the interactions between these species, and then focus on individual organisms, sensing the pace and rhythm of their lives. Finish by watching the grass grow, allowing your consciousness to resonate at the same pace.

721   **Loving creation** "Lord, may we love all your creation, all the Earth and every grain of sand in it. May we love every leaf, every ray of your light. For we acknowledge to you that all is like an ocean, all is flowing and blending, and that to withhold any measure of love from anything in your universe is to withhold that same measure from you."
FYODOR DOSTOYEVSKY (1821–81)

722 **Encounters with trees** "I frequently tramped eight or ten miles through the deepest snow to keep an appointment with a beech tree, or a yellow birch, or an old acquaintance among the pines." HENRY DAVID THOREAU (1817–62)

723 **Tree wisdom** Choose a tree that particularly appeals to you. Sit next to the tree and make friends with it. In silence ask it questions. Then wait for the responses to come to you: observe any words or images that arise within your mind.

If you lack certain qualities in your life, befriend a species of tree associated with those qualities. **Oak (724)** is associated with strength, **ash (725)** with peace and protection, **birch (726)** with healing, **cedar (727)** with courage, **cypress (728)** with comfort and the ability to cope with loss, **elder (729)** with acceptance of change, **maple (730)** with longevity, **pear (731)** with clarity, and **willow (732)** with overcoming depression.

733   **Whale song**   Play a CD of whale song. As you listen allow the calling of the whales to bring you into harmony with nature. Alternatively, listen to a CD of **rainforest sounds (734).**

735   **Meditate on a flower**   Get a sense of the overall pattern of the flower by scanning its main features. Do not attempt to find meaning in the pattern, simply allow the shapes, lines and hues of the petals to fill your consciousness, aware that the image is both in front of you and inside your mind. If the flower is fragrant, close your eyes and smell the perfume. Drinking in the essence of a flower in this way is deeply refreshing.

     Composite flowers (736) such as gerberas and chrysanthemums have many petals arranged into concentric patterns that provide natural mandalas for meditation.

737   **Perfect shade** "To sit in the shade on a fine day and look upon verdure is the most perfect refreshment." JANE AUSTEN (1775–1817)

738   **Balloon ascent** Imagine yourself in a hot-air balloon in a wilderness landscape, such as the rocky desert of Arizona or the steep mountains of the Pyrenees. As you rise in the balloon, a panoramic view unfolds around you. Visualize this view in all its details. Soon you are above the highest peaks, observing a terrain of spectacular beauty. You can make out distant coastlines, even the gentle curve of the Earth. Clouds pass below you. You still feel the Earth's gravitational pull but you are also aware of being on the edge of space. As you descend again, you acknowledge the immense privilege of being part of the natural scene below you, as it gets closer and closer, bigger and bigger – a giant sheet laden with gifts for you to enjoy.

739 **Nature's peace** "Climb the mountains and get their good tidings. Nature's peace will flow into you as sunshine flows into trees. The winds will blow their own freshness into you ... while cares will drop off like autumn leaves." JOHN MUIR (1883–1914)

740 **The summit** In many traditions around the world, mountains have long been regarded as sacred places and are believed to possess powerful energies. A mountain summit is therefore an ideal place to meditate, because you are at the apex of that energy and are profoundly connected with both earth and sky, bringing you a sense of rootedness and transcendence.

741 **Rays of light** "Abiding in her magnificent shrine, Amaterasu shines her protecting rays far to the lands of the four corners, her radiant light bringing peace everywhere under the heavens." INSCRIPTION AT THE ISE SHRINE, JAPAN (REFERRING TO THE SUN GODDESS)

742   **A summer meditation** A warm summer's day provides
the perfect opportunity for a summer meditation. Sit outside
in the sun, on a chair or on the ground, with your eyes closed.
Feel the warmth bathing your body. Imagine the sun's energy
connecting with your solar plexus, recharging the yellow
manipura chakra that resides there. Now visualize a warm
yellow glow spreading outward from your solar plexus,
filling the rest of your body with energy and strength.

   This meditation can also be adapted to cheer you up on cold
days in winter. Instead of lying outside in the sun, lie down in

a warm room and **visualize the sun
(743)** beating down on you.

744   Animal qualities
Meditate on your best-loved animal.
What qualities of this animal do you
most admire – the grace of a cat, the
unconditional loving of a dog?
Imagine how you would feel if you

embodied these qualities. By repeating this visualization you may gradually come to inhabit those qualities you so admire.

745 **Rain relaxation** On a rainy day find a sheltered place outside in which to sit, or sit inside with the window open. Close your eyes and take a few deep breaths to ground yourself. As you become more present, tune into the natural sounds around you – the splashing of rain in puddles, the rustling of wet leaves, the singing of birds, the distant rush of cars on wet roads. Focus on these sounds for five minutes, allowing them to relax you.

746 **A sprinkling of snow** "An overnight sprinkling of snow – our doubts, chased away by morning as faith climbs even wintry skies." MODERN HAIKU FROM FRANCE

747 **Walk on the calm side** When your brain feels foggy and confused, taking a ten minute walk in quiet surroundings will help to clear your head. As you walk, make a conscious effort to breathe deeply, inhaling for two steps and exhaling for two

steps in order to regulate your breathing pattern. With each out-breath imagine that the clouds in your mind are gradually clearing. At end of your walk, take three deep breaths, and gently shake your head to clear any remaining mental fog.

748 **A swan's flight** In Western music and ballet, the swan is a symbol of masculine light and feminine beauty. Meditate on the swan's flight and its powerful braking action as it lands, webbed feet foremost, with a splash in a twilit lake. Draw strength from its decisiveness. Know that such strength has its own beauty.

749 **The boundless sky** Sit where you have an unrestricted view of the sky – outside if weather pemits. Gaze at it with softly focused eyes. (Do not look directly at the sun, or you may do serious harm to your eyes.) Imagine that all thoughts, sensations, habits, doubts and worries are dissolving into the vast openness. Whenever a thought arises, or there is tension in your body, imagine that with each breath more and more space gathers around the tension, until it disappears into the boundless sky.

THE WEB OF LIFE

750 **Seeing the miraculous** "The purpose of miracles is to teach us to see the miraculous everywhere." St Augustine (354–430)

751 **Perceive inscape** The nineteenth-century English poet Gerard Manley Hopkins attempted to reveal what he called "inscape" – the pattern of distinctive characteristics that constitute the individual essence of a thing. In your daily life take time to pause and absorb the inscape in the people and things you see around you. Try to move beyond superficialities to perceive the uniqueness of each thing. Appreciate this uniqueness as an expression of the spirit.

752 **Microcosm** "Nature will bear the closest inspection. She invites us to lay our eye level with her smallest leaf, and take an insect view of its plane." Henry David Thoreau (1817–62)

753 **The life-force** By meditating on things in a certain way, we can sometimes catch a glimpse of their aura. To try this focus your attention on a plant. Closely observe its shape and form.

Now shut your eyes and take several deep breaths. When you open your eyes, look for pulsing patterns of energy around the edge of the plant. Adjust your focus, allowing your imagination to play a little. With practice you may develop a form of inner seeing that allows you to see the life-force within living things.

754 The world's mystery "The true mystery of the world is the visible, not the invisible." OSCAR WILDE (1854–1900)

755 Sparks of creation In the shamanic tradition the sun and the earth are thought of as the god and goddess of creation. Use this meditation to make contact with their love and vitality. Close your eyes and visualize a spark of love move from the earth up into your heart. Now imagine a spark of love pass from the sun into your heart. Feel the two sparks of love from the earth and sun unite, giving you strength and courage.

756 Healing connections As conscious beings we exist in constant relationship to self, others, nature and the One. During the course of life, these connections can become fractured or distorted. Use your meditation as an opportunity to heal these relationships and thereby reconnect with the life-force. Close your eyes and offer acceptance to yourself, respect to everyone you know, gratitude to nature, and appreciation to the One.

757 Myself in the universe "In everything that moves through the universe, I see my own body, and in everything that governs the universe, my own soul." CHANG TSAI (1020–77)

758 The world soul Meditate on the Renaissance idea of a world soul, the *anima mundi*. Sense the poetic beauty of this concept, and recognize it as a valuable corrective to materialism – even if you doubt its literal truth. When we embrace this insight, we start to respect our world, both natural and social; when we neglect this wisdom, we experience "loss of soul", or ennui.

759 A prayer to Mother Earth "O Mother Earth, You are the earthly source of all existence. The fruits which You bear are the source of life for the Earth peoples. You are always watching over Your fruits as does a mother. May the steps which we take in life upon You be sacred and not weak." OGLALA SIOUX PRAYER

760   Universal kinship Meditate on your connection with the world around you: all you hear, see, smell and touch, including the air that passes into and out of your body. Recognize your inseparable fusion with all you experience – the world in you and you in the world. Feel kinship toward all creation.

761   The World Tree This is a symbol used in shamanic traditions to describe the web of life. It is depicted as a tree bearing leaves, blossom and fruit to represent every stage of life. The branches and roots interlink to create an endless cycle of energy. Meditate on the World Tree to ground yourself.

762   Sacred Earth "Every part of this Earth is sacred to my people. Every shining pine needle, every sandy shore, every mist in the dark wood, every clearing and humming insect is holy in the memory and experience of my people … ." CHIEF SEATHL (19TH CENTURY)

763 **Agreement with nature** "The goal of life is living in agreement with nature." ZENO OF CITIUM (c.335–c.263BCE)

764 **Trace the web** Although we may think of ourselves as independent beings, we are inextricably linked to one another and to our environment in a complex web of interactions. Imagine yourself poised in the middle of a web. Each thread represents a connection that anchors you to the life around you. Look along each thread in turn and appreciate the many ways in which you are connected to the world – through relationships, commitments, and so on. You inhabit and accept this network. You rejoice in your connections and especially their uniqueness

765 **A thousand threads** "We cannot live only for ourselves. A thousand fibers connect us with our fellow men; and

among those fibers, as sympathetic threads, our actions
run as causes, and they come back to us as effects."
HERMAN MELVILLE (1819–91)

766 From seed to table To gain an understanding of the
relationships between living things, meditate on a table. In your
mind's eye, trace back through the stages in the table's history.
Imagine the carpenter constructing the table out of wood, the
felled tree, the mature tree, the slender young sapling, and
the tiny seed. Now follow the journey in reverse – from seed
to table. Offer thanks to the tree which is now at your service.

767 Causes and effects "There is no result in nature without
a cause; understand the cause and you will not have
to experiment." LEONARDO DA VINCI (1452–1519)

768 Butterfly winds According to the old
adage, if a butterfly flaps its wings in Japan, there is a
hurricane in New York. In other words all events are

inextricably interconnected – an idea long upheld by Eastern mystics and supported by discoveries in quantum physics. Take a decision to remind yourself of the importance of the energy that you send out into the world; everything you do has repercussions on everything else. Then act accordingly.

769   **Grass angels** "Every blade of grass has its angel that bends over it and whispers, 'Grow, grow.'" *TALMUD* (3RD–6TH CENTURY)

770 **The fabric of life** In a garden or park, meditate on the role each living organism plays in sustaining the fabric of life within that area. For example, visualize trees dispensing oxygen for surrounding creatures to breathe; worms aerating the earth so that it may nurture plants; grass and berries feeding animals and birds. Feel a renewed sense of respect for all living things.

771 **Links in the chain** "Earthworms, though in appearance a small and despicable link in the chain of nature, yet, if lost, would make a lamentable chasm." GILBERT WHITE (1720–93)

772 **The scarab beetle** This insect is known for rolling large balls of dung into underground nests. The female lays an egg in each ball and when the larvae hatch, they feed upon the dung – transforming waste into life. Meditate on the example of the scarab beetle – a humble character playing a vital role.

773 **Renting the world** "The world was not left to us by our parents, it was lent to us by our children." AFRICAN PROVERB

774 Companionship in nature "I am no more lonely than the Mill Brook, or a weathercock, or the north star, or the south wind, or an April shower, or a January thaw, or the first spider in a new house." HENRY DAVID THOREAU (1817–62)

775 A healing vision Close your eyes and visualize the planet Earth. Trace the global wounds of war, famine, deforestation, urbanization, pollution. Now imagine the Earth enclosed in pure, white light that turns people's hearts to a pure, virtuous energy. Watch as the wounds begin the slow process of healing.

776 Light and air "For me, a landscape does not exist in its own right, as its appearance changes at every moment; but the surrounding atmosphere brings it to life – the light and the air which vary continually." CLAUDE MONET (1840–1926)

777 Cradling the Earth Astronauts who have seen Earth from afar have often spoken of the intense love inspired by the experience. Imagine that you are in orbit in a space capsule and through a porthole you see the planet with its oceans and continents. It seems fragile but cocooned in the love of all those who care for it. You vow that after your return to Earth you will speak of your love and encourage others to emulate it.

LOVING SERVICE

778 **A drop in the ocean** "We ourselves feel that what we are doing is just a drop in the ocean. But if that drop was not in the ocean, I think the ocean would be less because of that missing drop." MOTHER TERESA OF CALCUTTA (1910–97)

779 **A prayer for work** Before embarking upon the day's tasks, utter a brief prayer dedicated to your work. Acknowledge the value of your tasks, and offer gratitude for the opportunity to contribute something of value to the world. Ask for the skills and qualities that will enable you to perform the task to the best of your ability, and resolve to offer your services with love.

780 **Lift the burden** "No one is useless in this world who lightens the burden of it for anyone else." CHARLES DICKENS (1812–70)

781 **Reviving the heart** "I pray for spirit to revive my heart, to spark it with a relish for service. I hope that my desire to be a flame of love will spark other stalled souls to come alive, aflame with love themselves." MODERN AFFIRMATION

782   **The hope of the world** "A vision without a task is but a dream. A task without a vision is drudgery. A vision and a task is the hope of the world." FROM A CHURCH IN SUSSEX, ENGLAND (1730)

783   **A day of love** During your morning meditation preview your day: imagine yourself choosing love over fear in every situation you encounter. In the evening review the day, acknowledge your ability to offer love, and forgive yourself for any moments when you showed fear.

784   **Acting in love** "The days are of most profit to him who acts in love." TRADITIONAL JAINIST SAYING

785   **Form and function** Meditate on a functional object. As you contemplate the form of the implement, appreciate that it is uniquely shaped to its task. Now turn your attention to yourself. Consider your own unique qualities and talents. What are the tasks that you are best shaped for? It is in these areas that you will best be able to express your love.

786 The perfect vessel Imagine that you are a potter. With skill and dexterity you lovingly transform the lump of spinning clay into a beautiful vessel. You are proud of your work but know that without the gift of earth you could have done nothing.

787 Mindful chores In many monastic traditions doing humble household chores is seen as a service to God and a vital part of religious training. Performed with mindfulness your own domestic chores can likewise become a form of meditation. In giving your full attention to the task, you are expressing respect for the person you're doing the task for.

788 Inside your heart In Hindu mythology the monkey king Hanuman shows outstanding devotion to Rama, an incarnation

of the deity Vishnu. To prove his loyalty Hanuman opens his chest to reveal Rama and his wife Sita enthroned in his heart. During meditation examine your heart to find what is enthroned there. Dedicate your heart to the positive force of love.

Hanuman acts on his devotion by rescuing Sita from kidnappers. Consider what actions you can take to **put your love into practice (789)** in the world.

790 **Melting the soul** "Accustom yourself continually to make acts of love, for they enkindle and melt the soul." St Teresa of Ávila (1515–82)

791 **River of life** On its journey from mountains to ocean, the river cleanses and nourishes all that it touches in its path. During your morning meditation visualize the day stretching before you as such a journey. Foresee the people you encounter touched and nourished by your presence, words and actions.

In your evening meditation return humbly to the mountains. Here, **summon gratitude (792)** for your ability to serve others.

THE GLOBAL FAMILY

793 **Planting trees** "One generation plants the trees; another gets the shade." CHINESE PROVERB

794 **The blueprint for life** DNA (deoxyribonucleic acid) is a complex molecule containing the genetic information needed to build, control and maintain a living organism. It is found in all living cells and is the blueprint of life. DNA forms a double helix – a shape like a twisted ladder. Imagine standing at the bottom of your DNA ladder. In your mind begin to climb. On the first rung sense your connection with your parents, each of whom bequeathed to you copies of half of their DNA. On the next rung sense your connection with your grandparents, and on the next your great-grandparents. In this way trace your roots back through generations of ancestors to the very first humans. Feel a sense of continuity through the ages and your connection to everybody on Earth.

795 **Secret histories** "If we could read the secret history of our enemies we should find in each man's life sorrow and

suffering enough to disarm all hostility." Henry Wadsworth
Longfellow (1807–1882)

796 Patchwork pieces We are like the pieces of a patchwork
quilt: stitched together by the common threads of our humanity,
the unique hue of each person's square making its bold and
distinctive contribution to the whole.

797 Bread and water "Our bread and water are of one table:
the progeny of Adam are as a single soul." Muhammad Iqbal
(1877–1938)

798 A pomegranate Everybody has a unique perspective on life,
which may conflict with our own. Think of these perspectives
as the seeds in a pomegranate fruit – many tiny parts which
together form a unified whole.

799 Completion "The soul of each single one of us is sent in order
that the universe may be complete." Plotinus (205–270)

800 **Seeds of unity** Although the world is full of discord, there are also seeds of peace that scatter and take root in unexpected places. They even grow among the rubble of bomb sites. They grow where the heart is pure. Those who see them know that the world is a garden, not a wilderness.

801 **Lions and spiders** "When spiders unite, they can tie up a lion." ETHIOPIAN PROVERB

802 **The Hall of Peace** "If anyone throws a stone, may it be only to mark the limits of the new foundations – a great Hall of Peace in which we will all give thanks to the Merciful Lord." MODERN PRAYER FROM SRI LANKA

803 **The passionate ones** All around you there is passion. You see lovers in the throws of youthful infatuation, which they call passion. But you are aware too of true passion – the great depth and warmth of loving feeling that all good people extend to others, even strangers. You feel this passion warming your heart,

and know that many of these young lovers, when the time comes, will feel it too. You belong to the brotherhood and sisterhood of the world's passion. Rejoice in your membership of this contented guild.

804 **Singing in unison** "The more we let each voice sing out with its own true tone, the richer will be the diversity of the chant in unison." ANGELUS SILESIUS (1624–77)

805 **Inner beauty** Within each of us lies a potent spark of divinity. Meditation helps us to discover this spiritual energy in all those around us. Close your eyes and bring to mind someone you know and love. As you meditate on this person, reflect on the spiritual qualities that you recognize in them.

Now practise this technique with **those you dislike (806)**, to improve your relationship.

When you meet **strangers (807)**, look beyond superficial appearances to find their inner spiritual beauty.

808 **One family** Through meditation we can play a part in healing the false divisions of race, religion and nationality, which scar our world. Close your eyes and visualize yourself hovering above the Earth in an airship. Look out across the world in all four directions. Perceive the spiritual light emanating from all human beings across the globe. Acknowledge the intrinsic goodness of every spirit, and the individual journey each must make. Conclude with a vision of humanity as a single spiritual family.

809 **Earth-minding** "Even as a mother at the risk of her life would watch over her only child, so let us with boundless mind and goodwill survey the whole world." THE BUDDHA (C.563–C.460BCE)

810 **Love for a stranger** Take an atlas and choose a place at random from the index. Find that place on a globe or a map of the world. Imagine you are a high-powered telescope in space. Zoom in on your location. Picture it in your mind. If there are people, what do they look like? Visualize them. Send them your loving thoughts.

811 **Be kind** We all have the power to enrich the world around us with kindness. Kind words or actions are their own reward. They are beacons blazing brightly, sending a message to all – even when the kindness has been private and unobserved.

812 **Helping others** "It is one of the most beautiful compensations of life, that no man can sincerely try to help another without helping himself." RALPH WALDO EMERSON (1803–1882)

813 **Relieving suffering** "I do all I can to relieve suffering in the world, remembering to take care of myself so I can care for others." MODERN AFFIRMATION

814 **Transforming pain** The Buddhist practice of *tonglen* – literally, taking and giving – allows us to help heal the suffering in the world, transforming it through positive, loving thoughts. Sit quietly and think of a person in pain. As you inhale feel their distress as a heaviness in your body. As you exhale feel their suffering dissipating, leaving your body as light, clear, fresh air.

815   **The kingdom of the mind**   "First there must be order and harmony within your own mind. Then this order will spread to your family, then to the community, and finally to your entire kingdom. Only then can you have peace and harmony." CONFUCIUS (551–479BCE)

816   **Holding suffering**   This meditation opens your heart to all those who are suffering. Begin by slowing your breathing. Then bring your awareness to your heart. Visualize yourself reaching out to embrace all those suffering in the world – people stricken by sickness, war, loss, violence, or physical or emotional pain. Begin with family and friends, then acquaintances, and finally those you don't know. Continue to breathe deeply, holding yourself and the suffering world within your heart.

817   **Strength in unity**   "Two weaknesses leaning together constitute a strength. Therefore the one half of the world leaning against the other half becomes firm." LEONARDO DA VINCI (1452–1519)

818   **Global vision** Close your eyes and conjure a vision of the
world in which all pain, fear and suffering have been eradicated.
Imagine the powerless finding power, and all people uniting
in friendship with one another. Reflect deeply on this vision.
In cherishing the dream you are bringing it one thought closer.

819   **A chord of peace** "I send out love into the world to
strike the chord of peace – the universal music of the heart."
MODERN AFFIRMATION

820   **Circle of light** Practise this meditation as a group. Stand
in a circle holding hands. Together, visualize a column of light
in the middle. Take it in turns to call out the names of people in
need of healing. Collectively visualize these people entering the
column of light to be healed by your collective loving energies.

821   **A world of peace** "I am co-creating a world of peace,
caring and goodwill. No matter what happens, I choose to
be a channel of love." MODERN AFFIRMATION

822 **A winged embrace** Visualize the Earth – a delicate blue and green sphere, rotating within a vast universe. Out of the darkness emerges a beautiful white dove. With wings spread wide the dove enfolds the Earth in a tender embrace. It is a messenger from God, bringing a vision of peace to humankind.

823 **Harvesting** "Let us aim to harvest peace. Let us exhaust ourselves in ploughing the stony ground." MODERN AFFIRMATION

Time
passing

CHANGE AND TRANSITION

824 **Follow the Tao** *Tao* is a Chinese word meaning "the way"
or "the path". Taoism is an Eastern philosophy based on the
principle that life involves ceaseless movement from one form
to another. Problems arise when we attempt to resist or control
the natural pattern of change. Harmony can be restored by
following the *Tao* – that is, by "going with the flow", accepting
the ever-changing pattern of life without judgment or resistance.

825 **The river** "You cannot step twice into the same river, for other
waters are continually flowing in." HERACLITUS (c.540–c.480BCE)

826 **The bending reed** Taoism, as taught by the *Tao te Ching*,
advises strength in flexibility. Accept the constant flow of the
universe. Bend to nature. This is how the reed gains its strength
and avoids being broken by the river's current. Follow the
practice of *wu-wei*, or non-interference in nature.

827 **Accepting what is** "I bow to the cycle of cause and effect,
whatever happens. I rejoice in what is." MODERN AFFIRMATION

828 **Something new** "All things must change to something new, to something strange." HENRY WADSWORTH LONGFELLOW (1807–1882)

829 **Life's flow** Just as the laws of nature reign over all living things, our lives follow a natural pattern that is woven into the larger tapestry of creation. If you are unable to fulfil your wishes in a situation, it may be that you are swimming against the current. Try letting go and trusting in the natural flow of events. Whatever is yours will come to you in due course.

830 **Give up the struggle** Change comes most quickly when we give up struggling against who we are – for this is the one thing we cannot change.

831 **River of life** "Every day I ride the river of my life. Some days I race across rapids, expanding my abilities and sense of myself; some days I swim in quieter waters by the banks, observing and learning from the river as it flows past; some days I float in deep pools of stillness where I renew myself." MODERN AFFIRMATION

832 **Coming and going** "There is no real coming and going, for what is going if not coming?" SA'DI OF SHIRAZ (c.1213–91)

833 **The still centre** If you stood in the middle of a room holding a piece of paper with a square cut out of the middle, and you held the paper at arm's length and turned slowly on the spot, you could watch the room pass across the square as if you were watching a movie. Similarly, in your meditations see yourself as a point of stillness in a world that is constantly moving. This will help you to remain calm when those around you prefer agitation.

834 **A phoenix** "Torched in the light of my awareness, my false self crumbles. Phoenix-like I create myself anew." MODERN AFFIRMATION

835 **Pass through** "When the way comes to an end, then change – having changed, you pass through." I CHING (12TH CENTURY BCE)

836 **Metamorphosis** All through our lives, we experience a continual process of transformation. Visualizing the life-cycle of

a butterfly can help us to accept that such change is a natural
process of life. First imagine a larva hatching into a caterpillar.
Watch the caterpillar grow as it munches through leaves, then
spins a cocoon for itself. After some time you see movement in
the cocoon – a butterfly is emerging. You watch as the butterfly
stretches its wings and flutters away. You are touched by the
beauty and ingenuity of nature's changes.

837   **Seasonal cycles**   Bring to mind an image of your home
and its surrounding landscape or cityscape as it is now. Notice
the weather and whether or not there are leaves on the trees.
If there are people in your picture, what are they doing? Scroll
forward in time and watch the changes that occur with the
passing of the seasons. As you do so acknowledge the cyclical
patterns of nature. Surrender yourself to life's flow.

838   **Around the world**   Remember an important consequence
of the world's roundness – the fact that what you take for an
ending is also a beginning.

839 **Hermetic guidance** At certain periods in our lives we undergo significant changes – for example, when moving house or ending a relationship. During these times we often feel vulnerable and lost, uncertain how to move forward. It can help to request guidance during meditation from the Greek god Hermes, who is associated with change and transition. Conjure him in your mind and ask him to guide you through the change. Later, watch out for coincidences and surprises, which may indicate that he is guiding you along the path.

840 **The future** To some extent, our expectations influence what manifests in our lives. To encourage an abundant future, imagine looking through an open doorway onto a beautiful landscape.

The scene is rich with images of all that you hope to experience – perhaps doves symbolizing peace, a pair of swans symbolizing true love. Now imagine stepping through the doorway into the promising future you deserve.

841   **Discover the new**   Our willingness to grow and change is often hampered by our fear of the new. Imagine that you are a bird soaring high above the landscape. A valley lies below, and as you rise you see rolling hills and, in the distance, mountains. As you observe this unknown territory, let go of fear and feel joyful anticipation of the adventures yet to come.

842   **Step forward**   "I step forward into the future with faith and courage, confident in my ability to face whatever challenges come my way." MODERN AFFIRMATION

843   **The invisible One**   "Invisible is the One to mortal eyes, beyond thought and beyond change. Know that the One is, and cease from sorrow." BHAGAVAD GITA (1ST OR 2ND CENTURY)

844   **Sunset endings**   Meditating on the sunset can help us come to terms with the loss that we experience with endings. On a clear evening, find a place outside where you can watch the sunset. As the sun sinks in the West, surrender to the final moments of the day. Allow the warm tints of the sky to open your heart to the poignancy of parting. Take strength to bear the ending from the potency of the setting sun, knowing that after night will come the start of a new day.

   If you cannot watch the sunset outside, perform this exercise by **visualizing the sunset (845)** instead.

846   **Renewal**   "All changes, even the most longed for, have their melancholy; for what we leave behind us is a part of ourselves; we must die to one life before we can enter another."
ANATOLE FRANCE (1844–1924)

847   **Change**   "All things change, nothing perishes."
OVID (43BCE–17CE)

TIMELESSNESS

848 The endless knot This is a Celtic symbol for eternity, comprising an interlaced line without a starting-point. When we meditate on this symbol, we capture a glimpse of the endlessness of time and the immortality of the spirit. As you focus on the image, allow these concepts to seep into your consciousness.

849 Above the precipice "I stand with exceeding care even on an ordinary cliff. How much more so above a precipice of a thousand leagues through the great expanses of time?" SHANTIDEVA (7TH CENTURY)

850 Time, the cook "Time of its own power cooks all beings within itself. No one, however, knows that in which Time itself is being cooked." MAHABHARATA (C.400CE)

851 The perpetual present Everything you will ever need can be found in the here and now of the perpetual present.

852   **The narrow gate** Every second of time is the narrow gate
through which enlightenment might enter.

853   **The hourglass** This is a symbol of the fluid nature of time. As
you see the sand pouring from the upper chamber to the lower,
meditate on the elusive nature of the
moment. Time is nature's method of
preventing everything from happening
at once. The way to wholeness is to
embrace the moment as it flies.

854   **Meditate on a clock face**
Gradually allow the image of the clock
to fill your consciousness. Become aware
of the ticking of the second hand. Shift your awareness to the
spaces between the ticks – a timeless realm where there is no
past, no future: only the present.

Apply this technique to your **thoughts (855)**. Watch the flow
of thoughts; then shift your attention to the spaces in-between.

856 River of time "To become enlightened you must cross the river of time. All material things pass away, but enlightenment lasts for all eternity." *DHAMMAPADA*, PART OF THE *PALI CANON* (C.500BCE–0)

857 Take control Perform this exercise to calm anxiety when you feel like you are running out of time. Begin by saying "stop" and pausing from your activity. Breathe in slowly and deeply. As you exhale imagine that time is expanding. Repeat this with your next two breaths, each time spending a little longer on the out-breath. You can now resume your task with a more focused mind.

858 An inch of time "An inch of time is worth an inch of gold. But an inch of gold cannot buy an inch of time." CHINESE PROVERB

859 **Beyond time** Practise this meditation to catch a glimpse of a timeless realm. Begin by observing the stream of thoughts passing through your consciousness. Pay attention to the spaces between thoughts until the spaces begin to expand. Practise shifting your awareness between the thoughts and the spaces. As you do so feel the thoughts begin to slow. Perform this exercise each day for five minutes. In time you may experience occasional moments of an absolute stillness beyond time.

GROWING OLDER

860 **A beautiful life** As we grow
older we may experience
sadness as our youth slips
away and the signs of aging
begin to accumulate. To come
to terms with this experience,
think of the cycle of the sun as
a metaphor for human life. As

you do so recognize that the beauty of life lies in its unfolding.
From birth until death we follow a beautiful curve of the spirit –
a transition from an innocent joy to a mature courage, which
has no truck with regrets.

861 **The erosions of time** Meditate on a lump of driftwood. As
you gaze upon its form, appreciate the beautiful erosions and
witherings of time and imagine the history that lies behind
them. Turn your attention to the marks that time has left upon
you. Recall the stories behind those marks, and the wisdom you
have accumulated along the way.

862 **Just listen** "Time gives good advice." MALTESE PROVERB

863 **Tower of wisdom** Gain strength and dignity from your wisdom. As the years settle on our heads like snow, the innocence and energy of youth

is replaced by the wisdom and perspective of experience. Imagine yourself in a tower full of books containing all the wisdom that you have acquired over the years. What are the titles of these books? What illustrations do they contain? Draw a sense of depth and strength from this tower of wisdom.

864 **Life counts** "And in the end, it's not the years in your life that count. It's the life in your years." ABRAHAM LINCOLN (1809–1865)

865 **One-way stream** Peace is the one-way flow of time without any ripple of regret or hindrance.

866 **Shedding antlers** Each October stags shed their antlers to grow a new pair. By mid-February the regrowth is complete, ready for the rut in April when stags battle to win access to the hinds (female deer). Throughout life we too shed aspects of ourselves. Like the stag we may feel bereft of our strength during this process of change. But, if we are patient during this vulnerable period, new strengths – new antlers – begin to emerge as alternative identities begin to form.

867 **Climbing the ladder** Every so often it is important to reflect on the journey so far, celebrating every step we have taken, every rung on the ladder. Even parts of our lives that we would prefer to forget (perhaps especially those parts) hold nuggets of gold among the dross – valuable lessons that we can use to help us in the present.

868   Second childhood "With a gentle hand I release regret. With acceptance I acknowledge lessons learned. With gratitude I give thanks for the richness of my experience. With a generous heart I share the treasures of my wisdom. Thus I enter the final chapter of my life as if it was the first. My gentleness, surrender, gratitude and generosity have given me back my childhood." MODERN AFFIRMATION

869   The bridge "The world is a bridge. Pass over it. Do not build your dwelling there." INSCRIPTION ON THE GREAT MOSQUE IN FATEHPUR SIKRI, INDIA (17TH CENTURY)

870   The nobility of aging As you lose your youthful strength, and your body acquires a more "lived-in" look, meditate on your true self, your essential consciousness. Body-consciousness has no place in your thoughts. You are old enough to know what really matters.

FACING MORTALITY

871   **A morning star** "The light which puts out our eyes is darkness to us. Only that day dawns to which we are awake. There is more day to dawn. The sun is but a morning star." HENRY DAVID THOREAU (1817–62)

872   **A new road** The poet Emily Dickinson described dying as "a wild night and a new road". If we thought we would live forever, we would feel trapped in our lives. The end is the ultimate relaxation: imagine yourself in your last moments letting go with a prayer of thanks for the life that was granted to you.

873   **Spiritual beings** "The key to a fulfilled life, without fear of death, is to appreciate that we are spiritual beings having a physical experience, rather than physical beings having a spiritual experience." PROVERBIAL WISDOM

874   **The washerwoman** In the Celtic tradition death is associated with Hallowe'en when the Great Mother is said to call her children home. One of the images of the Great Mother is of

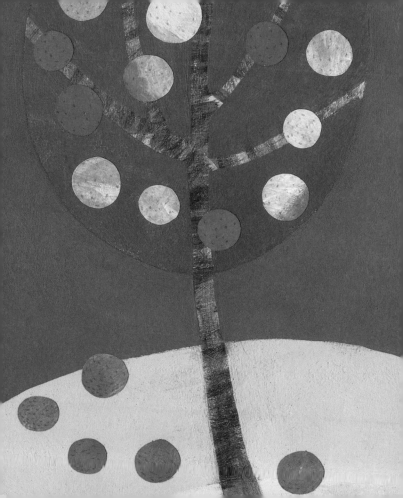

a woman washing clothes at a ford. Imagine standing before the washerwoman. You ask her whose clothes she is washing and she tells you they are yours. Fearfully you ask her if it is your time to die. Smiling, she replies that she hasn't finished your washing yet, but that, when your time comes, she will be there to guide you across the waters into paradise. You feel comforted, knowing that she will help you make the crossing.

875 The price of life "When you die, it will not be because you are sick, but because you were alive." SENECA (C.4BCE–65CE)

876 Immortal spirit According to many spiritual traditions, we are in essence pure spirit, and therefore immortal. One way to explore this idea is through meditation. Close your eyes and bring your awareness to yourself – the conscious being that animates your body. What you feel as you sit at peace with yourself is your own immortality. Visualize your spirit as a voyager, able to leave and enter your body at will. Think of death as merely a rite of passage, a moment of transition.

877   **A bird of spirit**   "The spirit looks upon the dust/ That fastened it so long/ With indignation,/ As a Bird Defrauded of its song." EMILY DICKINSON (1830–86)

878   **United once again**   "What bliss! At last I reach the shores of death – the place where rivers meet the ocean and souls reunite with the Source." MODERN AFFIRMATION

879   **The seen between unseens**   "Invisible before birth are all beings and after death invisible again. They are seen between two unseens. Why in this truth find sorrow?" *BHAGAVAD GITA* (1ST OR 2ND CENTURY)

880   **The homecoming**   "When the time comes, I will know that death is a homecoming, not a wrench that leaves a bruise on my spirit. Death is not the shadow but the light beyond the shadow. My spirit will return to its resting place in a long, slow glide toward peace." MODERN MEDITATION FROM ORKNEY, SCOTLAND

What really matters

TRUTH

881 **Knowing the Self** "Truth is exact correspondance with reality. For men and women, truth is the unshakeable knowledge of their real nature, the Self." PARAMAHANSA YOGANANDA (1893–1952)

882 **The true self** The Indian sage Ramana Maharshi often pointed out that as children we have a natural sense of "I am". To discover the true self, sit quietly and ask youself "Who am I?" As you reflect on this question, you may find that a palpable sense of "I am" begins to emerge in your consciousness.

883 **Restore truth** Our ability to perceive truth is often distorted by our beliefs. To raise awareness of your beliefs, meditate on a recent situation. Try to identify the beliefs that led to your actions. Now cast your mind back to your early years to learn the origins of these beliefs – perhaps in the messages given by parents and teachers. The greater your awareness of distorting beliefs, the more you will be able to perceive the truth.

In a similar way, meditate on the **actions of a colleague or partner (884)** to gain greater understanding of their behaviour.

885 **Look here** "If you cannot find the truth right where you are, where else do you expect to find it?" DOGEN (1200–1253)

886 **Three constants** Truth is that which never changes. In particular the three absolute constants are the self, God, and the dance of life. Meditate upon each to reconnect with truth.

The self is a still point of spiritual energy known as the soul. To meditate on this visualize **a point of light (887)** in the middle of your forehead, immediately above your eyebrows.

God is an ocean of unlimited peace, love and truth. To meditate on God, visualize your point of light rising up out of your body to connect with **an infinite expanse of light (888)**.

From this vantage point meditate on the **pattern of events (889)** on Earth – the dance of life – as it unfolds over time.

890 The dark moon According to pagan tradition the period
of the dark moon – when the moon is not visible in the sky – is
an ideal time for turning our attention inward in search of inner
truths. During this period take time to be alone with yourself.
Quiet your mind so that the voice of truth can be heard.

891 Through the maze Labyrinths symbolize the journey toward
spiritual truth. Visualize yourself walking slowly through a maze.
As you make each turn, imagine that you are shedding worldly
attachments. When you reach the heart of the maze, you feel
purified and renewed.
Stay a while before
retracing your
steps to rejoin
the world.

892 **Identity** "I have a body but am not my body. I have a mind but I am not my mind. I have thoughts but I am not my thoughts." MODERN AFFIRMATION

893 **Butterfly or man?** Zen master Chuang Tzu awoke from a dream of himself as a butterfly – or was he a butterfly dreaming that he was a man? When you meditate let go of concepts, ideas, thoughts and emotions, and simply be. In doing so you allow a greater understanding to dawn.

894 **Dreaming** "The world is as you dream it." SHAMANIC SAYING

895 **Solitude and connection** "It is when I am simultaneously aware of both my solitude and my deep connection with others that I sense the truth." MODERN AFFIRMATION

896 **Start with doubting** "The beginning of wisdom is found in doubting; by doubting we come to the question, and by seeking we may come upon the truth." PIERRE ABÉLARD (1079–1142)

897 **Seeing in the dark** "Unto this darkness, which is beyond light, we pray that we may come, and through loss of sight and knowledge may see and know that which transcends sight and knowledge, by the very fact of not seeing and knowing – for this is real sight and knowledge." DIONYSIUS (c.500CE)

898 **Solve a koan** In Zen Buddhism pupils are encouraged to meditate upon koans – paradoxical questions that cannot be answered logically. Practise this type of meditation to develop detachment from your mind. To begin, bring to mind the well-known koan: "What is the sound of one hand clapping?" Allow the question to fill your consciousness, and observe the failures of your mind to resolve the question with logic.

899 **Stay in the valley** "Truth is not always in a well. In fact, as regards the more important knowledge, I do believe that she is invariably superficial. The depth lies in the valley, where we seek her, and not upon the mountain-tops where she is found." EDGAR ALLAN POE (1809–1849)

900 Cleansing the doors of perception "When the doors of perception are cleansed, man will see things as they truly are, infinite." WILLIAM BLAKE (1757–1827)

901 Beyond the palette Imagine a palette containing all the hues of the rainbow. It would be easy to think that these are all the shades imaginable. Yet gold and silver are not among them. Likewise, all we can imagine can never be the whole of reality. Think of the divine as a hue that we have never perceived directly – only intuited.

902 On the seashore "To myself I seem to have been only like a boy playing on the seashore, diverting myself in now and then finding a smoother pebble or a prettier shell than ordinary, whilst the great ocean of truth lay all undiscovered before me." SIR ISAAC NEWTON (1642–1727)

903 The three candles "Three candles dispel the darkness: truth, knowledge, and the ways of nature." CHINESE PROVERB

904   **The awakening**   How near the truth is, yet how far away we search for it. Like fish unaware that they are swimming in water, we fail to realize we are immersed in spirit. Contemplate this idea in the stillness of your meditation practice. With time you may perceive the presence of the spirit as the veils of illusion lift.

905   **The ocean of Truth**   "If you would swim on the bosom of the ocean of Truth, you must reduce yourself to a zero."
MAHATMA GANDHI (1869–1948)

906   **Plato's cave**   The Greek philosopher Plato used the image of a person in a cave to illustrate our entrapment in the material world. Sitting in the cave we see shadows on the walls – the forms of the material world. On the evidence of our senses, we believe these shadows to be the reality, whereas in fact the true forms, which are casting the shadows, lie elsewhere.

907   **Finding peace**   To find peace we must look for real truths and love them when we find them.

908 Across the bridge "Go to the truth beyond the mind. Love is the bridge." STEPHEN LEVINE (20TH CENTURY)

909 The jungle The way is entangled by fears, doubts, errors and attachments. There is jungle all around us – but the machete of truth can be summoned in a moment to start cutting through the undergrowth of illusion.

COMPASSION

910 Evoke compassion When people harm others, it is tempting to condemn them for their actions, little realizing that this response is harmful to ourselves. Use meditation to evoke compassion. First bring to mind someone who wishes to harm others. Reflect that it is not them but their actions that are wrong. Understand that these actions are born out of their own inner pain. Feel compassion for their sufferings and visualize a healing light around their soul. You are healed in the process.

911 The strings of an instrument "I am spacious yet full of loving kindness; full of compassion, yet serene. I live like the strings of a fine instrument – not too taut but not too loose."
MODERN AFFIRMATION

912 Tapestries Our lives are like tapestries – each one of us unique and distinct, yet woven from common threads. The presence of these threads in all of us enables us to know each other as ourselves – and therefore to show compassion.

913 **Spiritual union** "When a person responds to the joys and sorrows of others as though they were his own, he or she has attained the highest spiritual union." *BHAGAVAD GITA* (1ST OR 2ND CENTURY)

914 **Open the heart** This meditation opens the *anahata* (heart) *chakra*, expanding our capacity for compassion. **1** Close your eyes and focus on the middle of your chest. **2** As you inhale visualize your heart expanding with the radiant light of love. **3** As you exhale visualize this light radiating from your heart into the world. **4** Continue this visualization for a few minutes.

915 **Another myself** "I will cease to live as a self and will take as my self my fellow creatures." *SHANTIDEVA* (7TH CENTURY)

916 **Easing distress** When we encounter suffering it is tempting to think there is nothing we can do. But in time we see other possibilities. To be compassionate we do not have to "fix" others' lives, or change the world. We merely have to open our hearts.

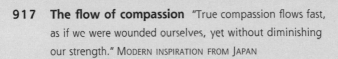

917 The flow of compassion "True compassion flows fast, as if we were wounded ourselves, yet without diminishing our strength." MODERN INSPIRATION FROM JAPAN

918 Lend your ear "Let your soul lend its ear to every cry of pain as a lotus bares its heart to drink the morning sun. Let not the fierce sun dry one tear of pain before you yourself have wiped it from the sufferer's eye. But let each burning human tear fall on your heart and there remain, nor ever brush it off until the pain that caused it is removed." TRADITIONAL VEDIC MEDITATION

919 True compassion To have compassion for the weakness we see in others, we must recognize and have compassion for the weakness within ourselves.

920 Enter Paradise "You shall not enter Paradise until you have faith, and you cannot have faith until you love one another. Have compassion on those you can see, and He whom you cannot see will have compassion on you." HADITH (7TH CENTURY)

LOVE

921 **A direction** "It is necessary to know only that love is a direction, rather than a state of the soul." SIMONE WEIL (1909–1943)

922 **Night owl** Imagine an owl hunting in the night, while you lie in bed asleep. Darkness blankets the woods, fields and marshes where it forages, yet for the owl it is daylight. Likewise, in these benighted times, you and your fellow seekers see clearly and your aim is true. Unerringly you find value in love and the spirit.

923 **See clearly** "And now here is my secret, a very simple secret: it is only with the heart that one can see clearly; what is essential is invisible to the eye." ANTOINE DE SAINT-EXUPÉRY (1900–1944)

924 **The light of love** Love is the sun. Without it, we stumble in darkness. It is love that makes all of us grow.

925 **Alive to love** "Peace and love are always alive in us, but we are not always alive to peace and love." JULIAN OF NORWICH (1342–c.1416)

926 **The fortress** Love is like a fortress at the top of a hill – it is built to weather even the most violent of storms.

927 **A butterfly** Visualize a butterfly inside of your heart. Gently it opens its wings, revealing its beauty. Breathing deeply and slowly imagine each breath flowing into the butterfly, strengthening your love and compassion for it. Continue for about five minutes. Practise this meditation regularly to encourage your heart to open to the world.

928 **Heart space** "A little space within the heart is as great as this vast universe." UPANISHADS (c.1000BCE)

929   **The oxygen of love**   Love is the oxygen of the spirit. It allows us to breathe. And it purifies, energizes and uplifts all that it touches.

930   **A beating heart**   "Of all the earthly music, that which reaches farthest into heaven is the beating of a truly loving heart." Henry Ward Beecher (1813–87)

931   **The flowering of enlightenment**   Self is the root, peace is the stem, love is the flower. Root, stem and flower are one. This is enlightenment.

932   **God's image**   "Love is an image of God – not a lifeless image, but the living essence of the all-divine nature which shines full of goodness." MARTIN LUTHER (1483–1546)

933   **Loving-kindness**   The practice of *metta*, or loving-kindness, fosters unconditional friendliness toward the self and others. In this abbreviated version of the traditional form, send *metta* to

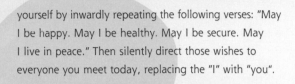

yourself by inwardly repeating the following verses: "May I be happy. May I be healthy. May I be secure. May I live in peace." Then silently direct those wishes to everyone you meet today, replacing the "I" with "you".

934 **Carving God's name** "I am in love and want the world to see. I have carved the many names of God onto all the trees within the sacred grove of my heart from which His music plays." FROM A FOLK SONG, SENEGAL

935 **The palm of the divine** Close your eyes and imagine that before you is a large upturned palm. You climb onto the softly cushioned palm and curl up in the middle. The hand closes protectively around you, rocking you back and forth. You feel warm, safe and loved.

936 **A little pencil** "I am a little pencil in the hand of a writing God who is sending a love letter to the world." MOTHER TERESA OF CALCUTTA (1910–97)

SPIRIT

937   **Trust the spirit**   There is an eternal life energy, a vital
principle that animates all of us. Different spiritual traditions
express this belief in different ways: some speak of the spirit,
some of God, some of the One. Essentially all these traditions
agree that the spirit is the source of all our love, all that we are.
Trust the spirit and you will discover not merely that such trust
is justified: it is the only thing that makes real sense of our lives
and creates true joy, whatever our circumstances.

938   **A string of planets**   "There is a secret One inside us; the
planets in all the galaxies pass through his hands like beads –
that is a string of beads one should look at with luminous
eyes." KABIR (1440–1518)

939   **Trinity of the spirit**   Our spirit has three essential functions –
to destroy, create and sustain. Exercising these capacities during
meditation provides the means for self-transformation. First
reflect on a positive quality you would like to develop, such as
peace. Now visualize as weeds the emotions that are disrupting

your peace – they are growing in the soil of your consciousness. Imagine pulling up these weeds and burning them in the fire of love. Take the ashes of the weeds and spread them across the soil. Then plant seeds of calm and watch as they begin to take root and grow, nourished by the ashes of the burnt weeds.

940 **True being** "The whole of existence is imagination within imagination, while true being is God alone." IBN AL'ARABI (1165–1240)

941 **Thirsty fish** "I laugh when I hear that the fish in the water is thirsty. I laugh when I hear that men go on pilgrimage to find God." KABIR (1440–1518)

942 **The music of silence** Sit comfortably in a quiet place with your eyes shut, taking slow, deep breaths. Listen intently to all the quiet noises you can hear – if only the wind outside, or the creaking of the house. Listen too to your own breathing. Imagine these sounds blending together into a vast, subtle symphony. This is one of the quiet passages in the music of your life. Relish this music as a gift to your spirit.

943 **Spirit singing** The life-force (known as *prana* in the Vedic tradition) is often associated with the breath. Improvised singing can therefore be a powerful way to contact and express your spirit – the life-force within you. Find a place where you can make noise without being disturbed. Stand with your arms by your sides and your feet apart. Take a deep breath and push air through your mouth to create a sound. Do not try to form words or a tune. The aim is not to make beautiful sounds but to express your spirit through your voice. Be aware of your feelings, giving them full vocal expression in all their rawness and power.

944 Finding spirit "I close my eyes and look within. At the centre of my being I see a still point of light – radiant and pure. It is my spirit, the alpha and omega of my life." MODERN AFFIRMATION

945 A cleansing rush of water Beautiful music is a cleansing rush of water through the pipework of the spirit. It leaves you fresh and wide awake. Your energies flow freely and lovingly.

946 Birth of a whisper "Could it be that my whisper was already born before my lips?" OSIP MANDELSHTAM (1891–1938)

947 Chanting "OM" According to Vedic scripture OM is the primordial sound from which the entire universe was created. Using "OM" as a mantra connects us with the source of the universe. While chanting this mantra hold the sound for as long as possible, paying attention to the experience of the vibrations as they reverberate through your body.

Alternatively, chant **"one" (948)**, **"peace" (949)**, or any other **word with particular resonance (950)** for you.

951 **Spiritual fruits** The Sufis – Persian mystics – believed that knowledge without practice is like a tree that bears no fruit. Experience your practice of meditation as a guarantee of inner fruitfulness, an important step toward your spiritual harvest.

952 **Oil and butter** "Like oil in sesame seeds, like butter in cream, like water in springs … so dwells the Lord of Love, the Self, in the very depths of consciousness. Realize him through truth and meditation." *UPANISHADS* (c.1000BCE)

953 **The wheel of law** The Hindu symbol of the *chakravartin* – the wheel of law – symbolizes movement and completeness. See the wheel as a representation of yourself: the hub is your true nature; the spokes are aspects of your personality; the outer rim is your worldly form. Focus on how the hub holds the wheel together. Then meditate on the central point – your divine spirit.

954 **Faith** "Gratefully I put my faith in the spirit. Here I find peace and the strength to deal with any adversity." MODERN AFFIRMATION

955 **A grain of rice** "This is the spirit that is in my heart, smaller than a grain of rice ... or a grain of canary-seed, or the kernel of a grain of canary-seed; this is the spirit that is in my heart, greater than the Earth ... greater than heaven itself, greater than all these worlds." *UPANISHADS* (C.1000BCE)

956 **The Bodhi tree** According to tradition the Buddha reached enlightenment under a banyam, which became known as the

Bodhi ("enlightened") tree. The Bodhi tree rejuvenates itself by
rooting its branches in the soil. It symbolizes the immortality of
the spirit. Imagine sitting beneath a Bodhi tree. Gazing upon the
long, extended branches, be aware of your own spirit, existing
in countless incarnations past, present and future.

957 **Changeless spirit** "I rejoice in the spirit, which is changeless.
I am happy in my loving independence of the material
world." MODERN AFFIRMATION

958 **Expand your spirit** Religious traditions from all
around the world use light as a symbol for the spirit. We
can use this image to contact the spirit within ourselves. Sit
comfortably, close your eyes and draw a few deep breaths.
Next time you inhale imagine a point of light at the core of
your being, exuding brilliant white energy. On every inhalation
imagine this light growing brighter and radiating out further
from your inner self until it extends into every part of your
body. Continue to meditate on this white light for about five

minutes. At the end of the
meditation, bow your head
toward your chest and gently
open your eyes.

959 **Your inner sanctuary** This
is a place inside where you can
go to reconnect with your spirit.
Close your eyes and visualize a
tranquil landscape. In this place,
imagine building a sanctuary
that reflects the beauty of your
spirit. The materials you require
appear as if by magic. Once
you have built, decorated and
furnished your sanctuary, sit for
a few moments inside. Feel
peace descend as you connect
with yourself once more.

960   **Knowledge of the spirit** "By meditation upon light and upon radiance, knowledge of the spirit can be reached and peace can be achieved." PATANJALI (2ND CENTURY BCE)

961   **Pioneers of pain** Pain creates new territory for the spirit. We are all pioneers of pain. Our lives on the frontier are the history of our people.

962   **Darkness of the night** "Even though the night darkens your spirit, its purpose is to impart light. Even though it humbles you, revealing the depth of your wretchedness, its purpose is to exalt and uplift you. Even though it empties you of all feeling and detaches you from all natural pleasures, its purpose is to fill you with spiritual joy and attach you to the source of that joy." ST JOHN OF THE CROSS (1542–91)

963   **Your spiritual friend** We know the spirit by names, such as Beloved or the Source, but it is hard to give it an actual shape. Imagine the spirit as a loving friend. If your spiritual friend wrote you a letter, what would the letter say? How would your friend's love be expressed? Find a quiet place to write this letter, and keep it for times when your friend seems far away.

964   **Prayer**   "Prayer is an intimate friendship, a frequent conversation held alone with the Beloved." St Teresa of Ávila (1515–82)

965   **Spiritual fertilizer**   Without the spirit, knowledge would never flower into wisdom and incident would never flower into experience.

966   **Breath of God**   Abbess Hildegard of Bingen, a wise mystic of the Middle Ages, told the story of a king who raised a feather from the ground and commanded it to fly. The feather flew, not because of anything in itself, but because the air bore it along. "Thus am I,"

she said, "a feather on the breath of God." Have faith that you
too can allow the spirit to move you.

967 **Spiritual beauty** During meditation bring to mind someone
whose spiritual beauty has touched your heart. Recall the nature
of your encounter. What was the quality of their energy that
touched you? Remember that what you recognize in others, you
possess within yourself.

968 **Purity** "The purity men love is like the mists which envelop
the earth, and not like the azure ether beyond." HENRY DAVID
THOREAU (1817–62)

969 **The soaring balloon** Visualize a hot-air balloon tied to
the ground by ropes. The balloon represents your spirit; and the
ropes, your attachments. Visualize yourself untying each rope in
turn until the balloon lifts off the ground and your spirit is free
to soar. Remember that you are in charge of how high you wish
to go – simply adjust the flame or let go of some sandbags.

970 At ease "I live in the spirit, at ease with body and mind, with nature in its infinite richness, with others in spiritual kinship." MODERN AFFIRMATION

971 The dragon The Chinese dragon symbolizes joy, energy and health, and is often depicted as the guardian of spiritual wisdom. Meditate on this fabulous creature. Watch light play on the patterns of its hide; reach out to touch its glittering scales. Feel the energy of spirit in each rumbling dragon breath.

972 A leaping salmon "The spirit flashes, like a salmon leaping. Although a salmon may be caught on a hook, the fisherman has no way to capture its beauty." MODERN INSPIRATION FROM SCOTLAND

973 The Great Path "The Great Path has no gate. Thousands of roads enter it. When one passes through this gateless gate, one walks freely between heaven and earth." MUMON (1900–1988)

974   **Beyond words**   Be at one with all that is beyond definition.

975   **Two sides of a coin**   The spiritual and material realms are two sides of the same coin – each interpenetrates and is essential to the other. Through meditation we learn to balance our perceptions of material reality with a spiritual vision of interconnectedness, which we perceive intuitively. Seek to integrate both perspectives to create a holistic view of life.

976   **Two lamps**   "I am you, O God. ... Your soul and my soul are like two lamps, shedding a single light." AL HALLAJ (c.858–922)

977   **The five-pointed star**   The pentacle is a symbol of cosmic union, comprised of two interlocking triangles. The narrow triangle pointing upward indicates the masculine heaven principle; the wider, central triangle pointing downward, the feminine earth principle. Meditating on the pentacle aligns you with the cosmos, harmonizing the complementary energies of masculine and feminine within your nature.

978 The bell and the thunderbolt In Buddhist art and ritual, the bell is associated with the female principle, and compassion; while the thunderbolt is associated with the male principle, and wisdom. Compassion without wisdom is a bell without a clapper. Wisdom without compassion is a thunderbolt without rain.

979 The plan of the universe "Unity in variety is the plan of the universe." VIVEKANANDA (1863–1902)

980 Optical illusion Our separation from each other is the optical illusion of our consciousness.

981 The jewelled tower An ancient Eastern text called the *Avatamsaka Sutra* likens the universe to a vast jewelled tower containing an infinite number of identical vast jewelled towers. All is contained in one and each contains all. The universe is an interconnected whole, in which the properties of any one part are determined by those of all the others. In this sense every part contains the whole.

982　**The cardinal directions** Embrace the unity of the material world by meditating on a compass. First contemplate the points denoting North, South, East and West. Then move your focus to the intersection of the points, where all four become one.

983　**Yin and yang** The ancient Chinese *yin-yang* symbol conveys the idea of fundamental unity within all of creation, based on a dynamic interplay between complementary opposites. Hold in your mind the meaning of the symbolism: *yin* is feminine, dark, receptive and passive; *yang* is masculine, bright, expansive and active. Both are essential to our experience. Only through the interplay of difference can distinctions be made.

984　**Drops of honey** "As bees sip nectar from many flowers and make a hive of honey, so that not one drop can claim, 'I am from this flower or that,' all creatures, though one, do not realize that they are one." UPANISHADS (C.1000BCE)

985   Oneness and separation Consciousness of oneness requires experience of separation.

986   The Tree of Life In traditional Hebrew texts the Tree of Life embodies the soul's journey back to the source. The Tree reflects all the possibilities that are open to humankind and stands as an image of the entire universe. Meditate on the Tree to remind you of your spiritual purpose when your life seems off-track.

987   Desert islands We imagine ourselves alone – desert islands in a vast ocean. Yet when we look beneath the waves, we see that we all rise out of the same earth. We are connected at our roots.

988   Serve the Self "The soul who meditates on the Self is content to serve the Self and rests satisfied within the Self; there remains nothing more to accomplish." BHAGAVAD GITA (1ST OR 2ND CENTURY)

989   **The source of all movement** "I finally discovered the source of all movement, the unity from which all diversities of movement are born." ISADORA DUNCAN (1878–1927)

990   **The cosmic dancer** In the Hindu tradition Shiva is the god of creation and destruction who sustains the endless rhythm of the universe through his dance. He is often represented as a four-armed figure encircled by flames. Meditate on Shiva to see beyond the endless movement and change of the universe – of Shiva's cosmic dance – to the underlying oneness.

991   **Dance with life** Life is an experience of continuous change. Rather than resisting life's changes, dance with whatever happens and in doing so become one with the flux.

992   **Beyond duality** Close your eyes and imagine that you are climbing into a rocket. In an instant the rocket lifts you high above the Earth, beyond all duality. Looking down you see one world, one family of souls, all connected by the thread of love.

993   **The Lord of Love**   "All is change in the world of the senses, but changeless is the supreme Lord of Love. Meditate on him, be absorbed in him, wake up from this dream of separateness." *UPANISHADS* (C.1000BCE)

994   **A single drop**   Imagine you are a drop of water in the sea. There are billions of drops, and together you form an ocean. Now meditate on your own spirit. You are one among many, all unique yet alike in one thing: you share the spirit of the One.

995   **A grain of sand**   "To see a world in a grain of sand,/ And a heaven in a wild flower,/ Hold infinity in the palm of your hand,/ And eternity in an hour." WILLIAM BLAKE (1757–1827)

996   **The lotus of light**   The lotus is often associated with enlightenment. The leaves and flowers open at dawn and close at dusk, making this a perfect symbol of light. It grows in mud, demonstrating the transformation of impurity into purity. Meditate on the lotus. Let your spirit reach toward the light.

997 **A thousand petals** Realizing our connection with the Source is the aim of meditation. We can connect to the Source through the crown *chakra* – called the *sahasrara*, meaning "a thousand petals". The *sahasrara chakra* is depicted as a full-blossomed lotus radiating a thousand rays of light. Visualize this on the crown of your head as you meditate. This will lead you to a realization of your true self, and a oneness with the supreme consciousness.

998 **The goal of union** "When your mind, which may be wavering over the contradictions of many scriptures, shall rest unshaken in divine contemplation, then the goal of union is yours." *BHAGAVAD GITA* (1ST OR 2ND CENTURY)

999 **Meditate on a mandala** Mandalas are pictorial representations of the cosmos, usually consisting of a number of geometric shapes, organized in concentric circles. They are used in the Hindu and Buddhist traditions as an aid to meditation. Focus on the mandala, moving mentally toward its heart, in order to achieve a sense of oneness with the universe.

1000 Expansion As you meditate imagine your breath as an extension of your being. Let your perception expand, until you no longer exist in a defined space, but fill the entire universe.

1001 World flow "Whoever holds in their mind the great image of oneness, the world will come to them ... in safety, oneness and peace." LAO TZU (C.604–531BCE)